W9-CFS-428

City guide
MUNICH
up-to-date city guide of Munich

Photos: Reinhold Armbruster-Mayer, Ulm

Text: Wilhelm Rupprecht, Munich

"Grüß Gott" and welcome to Munich!

You have this book in your hands which means that you are already here or in your way, and maybe you have heard this or that about Munich: Maybe that Munich is the third largest city in Germany (after Berlin and Hamburg), but is number one when asked about the best-loved or the most attractive one.

Maybe that the "Münchners" are easy going people, who love to enjoy their beer but suffer, from time to time, of a local typical moodiness. That Munich is the home town of the Football Legends FC Bayern, "Monaco Franze" and the Oktoberfest; that the mountains and lakes of the Upper Bavaria reach almost the city and here the Föhn can occur at any time of the year and excuses any kind of nonsense.

Maybe that Munich is an important cultural center with numerous treasures concentrated mainly in three Museums: the Old and the New Pinakothek [B] as well as the Pinakothek der Moderne [25] from a cultural point of view a world record!

But these are just a couple of highlights. Maybe you would like to know more before you start your journey and with the help of this guide explore and discover the city:

Munich lies at about 500 meters above the sea level, on the shores of the river Isar, counts a population of around 1,2 million (in other days almost 1,4 million) and is the capital of the Free State of Bavaria, the largest state in extension of Germany. Until the half of the last century

Munich was known to be the "Farmers´ Metropolis", as the connections between the countryside and the city were very close and the city took profit of the constant migration of the farming population from the surroundings.

After the World War II the structure of the city changes: multinational companies settled their headquarters here and expanded, for example Siemens, MAN, BMW. By the end of the century developed to a communications and High Technology center. Two universities, several high schools (music, art) attract over 100 000 students – more than any other place in the Federal Republic of Germany. They feel attracted not only by the educative opportunities, but certainly as well by the excellent leisure possibilities of the city.

Starting with the lakes and parks in the city center, for example the English Garden [C] one of the largest and more beautiful parks in the whole world. For the sport and fitness life you find almost everything, in the south of the city the several lakes and mountains fascinate sailors and surfers, bikers and hikers and extreme athletes find their opportunities.

The high level cultural life can keep up with its reputation. The famous and highly subsidized federal and municipal theaters belong to the leading stages in the country, the numerous private and independent stages ensure the offer and the variety, the musical life is leaded mainly by three top orchestras: the Münchner Philharmoniker, The Orchestra of the Staatsoper [17] and the Bavarian Radio and

Television Orchestra, all of them with well known conductors. About the Pop and young cultural life the reputation of Munich was "sleepy". Since a couple of years this has change and the "youth under 50" wishes to find an attractive successor for their beloved Kunstpark Ost, maybe in the future Football stadium.

Munich is a city with plenty to see: the Residence [18] and the Nymphenburg Castle [113], museums, churches and other historical sites, with royal impressive avenues and Middle Ages city gates. But all these are not death memorials.

The "Münchners" live with them, integrating them in the normal day life, without fearing them. This easy-going way of life makes out of Munich a city with a peculiar flair, and gives the place the nickname "the most northen city of Italy".

But beware! Do not believe, if you come here for the first time, that the people in Munich live only under the moto "dolce far niente", sweet doing nothing. The economical power of the city – and its surrounding communities of the "Speck belt" – is to be regarded.

The growth is above the average of the Federal Republic, with the consequence of a higher cost of living, for example for property and lodging. Nobody gets things for free, neither "natives" nor "adopted". The majority must work hard in order to keep their standard of living, even though they don't let it show.

Of course there is a very special society of "wannabees", lazy noblemen, yuppies, the "kiss-society" about who you can read in the yellow press. But the majority of the people live under the motto "live and let live". That is the reason why the visitor feels here from the beginning like at home.

Brief History of the City.

10./11. Jh. On the banks of the Isar, monks from Tegernsee abbey establish a settlement called "Munichen". The municipal coat of arms recalls this origins depicting a monk: the "Münchner Kindl".

1158 Founding of the city by Heinrich the Lion, Duke of Bavaria and Saxony, he destroys the toll bridge over the Isar which existed where now the German Museum [9] stands. He establishes a town market and mint and ensures his income from the trade (Salt!).

1255 Munich becomes the main residence of the Wittelsbach, Dukes of Bavaria.

1293 Construction of the city fortification, today visible at the Karlstor [36], Sendlinger Gate [41], and Isartor [8].

1314-47 Reign of Ludwig "The Bavarian", from **1328** German Emperor.

1348 First Black plague in the city.

1385 The construction of the Residence [18] begins, in those days named Neuveste.

1468 First stone of the Cathedral Church of our Lady (Frauenkirche) [31] (**1494** finished).

1505 Munich becomes capital and main residence of the united Duchy of Bavaria.

1550-79 Duke Albrecht V, Counter Reformation in Bavaria.

1600 Building of the new Residence [18] under the ruling of the duke, later Elector Maximilian I Munich counts with around 20 000 inhabitants.

1632 Gustav Adolf of Schweden occupies Munich during the 30 Years War. Two years later one third of the population dies due to the plague.

1679-1726 Elector Max Emanuel, occupation of Munich by the Austrian troops (**1705-14**), peasants rising against the occupation forces (Sendlinger Christmas Massacre **1705**), Construction of the Nymphenburg [113] and Schleißheim castles.

1799-1825 Elector Max IV Joseph, from 1806 King of Bavaria "for the grace of Napoleon".

1810 First Oktoberfest on the occasion of the wedding of the Crown Prince.

1825-48 Ludwig I transforms Munich with many classical constructions (Ludwigstreet, Königsplatz [A]) into the "Athens by the Isar".

1848-64 Maximilian II, (Maximilianstreet, Maximilianeum [15])

1864-86 Ludwig II, the "Fairy Tale King", does not take care of the city, concentrates in the construction of his magnificent castles.

1886-1912 "Prince Regency" under Luitpold (1906 Founding of the German Museum [9]); "Munich flourishes".

1918/19 November Revolution, Resignation and fleed of Ludwig III, last ruler of the Wittelsbach dynasty. Munich proclaimed capital of the Free State of Bavaria.

1923 Failled Adolf Hitler's "Beer Hall Putsch [19]" on 9th Nov.

1933 Taken of the power by the national socialists in the Munich Town hall [2]; Construction of the concentration camp in Dachau.

1935 "Capital of the movement";

1938 "Munich Treaty" (Germany, Italy, France, Great Britain), division of Chekoslovaquia, last effort to maintain the peace.

1939-45 World War II, main part of the old town destroyed by the bombs; University resistance group "White Rose" with the sisters Scholl.

1957 Munich population reaches one million.

1972 The 20th Olympic games are held in Munich.

2002 The Football World Cup 2006 will take place in Munich; Inauguration of the Pinakothek der Moderne [25].

Walking tour of the Old town

Walking tour of the Old town – a stroll trough the historical center of the city

The heart of the city beats in the **Marienplatz** [1]. Here is the meeting place for the citizens of Munich, the tourist, the political events, festivity hall for the receptions of prominents such as the Chancellor or the football team FC Bayern. And it is nowadays not much different from the beginning, when the salt trade road between Salzburg and Augsburg, thanks to which the foundation of Munich happened, transformed right here in a wide square. In the Middle Ages this square was the place for musicians, tumblers, magicians and entertainers, and not much has change since then! The only thing that does not happen here any more, thanks heaven!, are the beheadings. The execution place disappeared long time ago.

This square owes its name to the **Mary Columm (Mariensäule)**, a 11 meters high work erected in 1638 in the middle of the place. The Elector Maximilian wanted to thank this way for the sparing of the city during the occupation by the Swedish troops of the King Gustav Adolf. The golden bronze statue of the Virgin Mary represents the Queen of Heaven on the moon with scepter, crown and child. This statue, work of Hubert Gerhart of 1590, originally intended for the Cathedral Church of Our Lady (Frauenkirche) [31] has turned now in to the symbol of the city. The four winged children on the pedestal fight against the plagues of humankind: famine,

Marienplatz [1] with the Mary Column and the Old City Hall [3] with Tower

New City Hall [2]

Carrillon

its 85 meters high tower the **Carillon (Glockenspiel)** (daily at 11 a. m., 12 a. m. and 5 p. m.). Its rotating figures present two scenes from the city history: the jousting tournament for the wedding of the Duke in 1568, and the cooper's dance (Schäfflertanz), reminder of the plague in the year 1517, as the barrel makers celebrated the end of the Black Death with this dance.

> It is possible to go up to the City Hall Tower:
> Mon - Fri 9 a.m. - 7 p.m., Sat, Sun, Hol
> 10 a.m. - 7 p.m.
> Nice view over the city and the background mountains.

war, heresy and black plague, symbolized by the dragon, the lion, the snake and the basilisk. In the **Fish Fountain (Fischbrunnen)**, restored in 1954 by Prof. Henselmann, the "Münchners" perform every ash Wednesday the tradition of washing the empty wallets after carnival.

At the east side of the Marienplatz [1] stands the **Old City Hall (Altes Rathaus)** [3], mostly a late gothic hall building, work of the cathedral architect Jörg von Halsbach, called Ganghofer, around the year 1470. Transformed several times with the passing of time, and damaged during the WW II had to be reconstructed, together with the attached tower. The Ball room with its beautiful timber barrel vaulting once used by the citizens of Munich for their festivities, is used nowadays only for representative events of the city.

The north side of the square is dominated by the **New City Hall (Neues Rathaus)** [2]. This in its days fashionable Flemish-Neo-Gothic style building was erected between 1867 and 1908 under the supervision of Georg Hauberrisser. Here "rule" the three Mayors and the City Parliament, known as City Council. Attracting the sight and the cameras of the tourists we find at

> Besides: Toy museum (Spielzeugmuseum) now housed in the Rathaus tower. A very interesting children's room is exhibited here. Daily. 10 a.m. - 5.30 p.m.

> **Tourist Information:**
> in the New City Hall, entrance Marienplatz Mon. - Fri. 10 a.m. - 8 p.m., Sat. 10 a.m. - 4 p.m. U-, S-Bahn Marienplatz.

Passing by the bookshop Hugendubel we leave behind the Marienplatz [1] and face immediately the church of **St. Peter (Peterskirche)** [4], the oldest and most popular house of God in Munich. The first construction in this place dates back to the 11th century, what we see nowadays is mostly a Gothic new construction of the 13th and late 14th century with posterior additions in Baroque and Rococo style.

One of the hidden treasures of St. Peter is the Baroque High altar with estatues of the four Church Fathers by Egid Quirin Asam (1732), topped by the expressive figure of St. Peter by Erasmus Grasser (1492). Also well worth seeing are the five pannels of Jan Pollack (1517) in the Choir, the beautiful Rococo choir stalls as well as the 20 altars (about 1400) showing the Last Judgement.

The damages of the war were such that the church should have been torn down. Very special is the tower of this church nicknamed the **"Old Peter" (Alter Peter)** [4] a landmark of special meaning for the people of Munich. For this reason became in the fifties the original

roofing with the form of 1607. Over 303 steps take to the **viewing plattform (Aussichtsgalerie)**. The climbing is rewarded by a dramatic view of Munich with its magnificent Alpine backdrop.

> **i** Mon - Sat 9 a.m. - 7 p.m.,
> Sun, Fri 10 a.m. - 6 p.m.

At the foot of the hill "Petersbergl", leading up to St. Peter (Peterskirche) [4], extends the oldest and largest farmer's market of Munich. The **Viktualienmarkt** [5]. In here you can enjoy a traditional atmosphere, mixture in between aepicurian friendliness and "Gemütlichkeit", with the touch of the earthy remarks of the market women. The butchers have their traditional row, the fishmongers their corner. Do not expect bargains here, the motto is: Quality has its price! The only thing for free is what the eyes and the nose can enjoy. The new comers are the beer garden, the maypole and six fountains which statues recall several popular folk singers, Karl Valentin, Liesl Karlstadt, Weiß Ferdl.

> **i** Mon-Sat 7:30 a.m. - 6 p.m.

Old Peter [4] with Alpine background

9

Old Peter [4], High altar of the church

Viktualienmarkt [5]

Excursion: the Gärtnerplatz quarter [6]

"Behind" the Viktualienmarkt [5] (when coming from the Marienplatz [1]) you end up in the **Gärtnerplatz Quarter** [6], here you will not find "Sights" as such, but a very lively young atmosphere with bars, cafes, terraces, small theatres, cinemas and multifunctional locals. Apparently this quarter homes the largest number of hairdressers in town. Take a stroll through the streets Reichenbach-, Rumford-, Buttermelcher-, Baader-, Klenze- und Hans-Sachs-Strasse and keep your eyes open!

From the east side of the Viktualienmarkt [5] we continue through the charming square Dreifaltigkeitsplatz and along the Heiliggeiststreet towards the Tal. We find at the corner of the street the Church of the **Holy Spirit (Heiliggeistkirche)** [7], once the oldest Gothic hall church in the city, suffered so much damage and fires that did

not adquire its Baroque form until after the war. Outstanding works in the church are the so-called Hammerthaler Mother of God in the altar dedicated to Mary (about 1450) and the late Gothic cross (1510) in the Cross chapel.

Fountain dedicated to Karl Valentin [5]

Church of the Holy Spirit [7]

Excursion: Tal, German Museum [9], Cultural Center Gasteig [11]

The **Tal** is what remains of the oldest Crossroads of Munich, when the transport of salt from Salzburg to Augsburg passed through here. The importance of the old days can be traced back in the still existing hotels and inns where just about 100 years ago the horse carriages made their stop over. The **Isar Gate (Isartor)** [8] at the end of the street was the eastern boundary of the city fortifications at the times of Ludwig the Bavarian (about 1330).

When restored 170 years ago adquired the wall-painting depicting the triumphal entry of Emperor Ludwig the Bavarian after the battle of Mühldorf (1322). The **Valentin-Musäum** situated in the Gate is dedicated

to the wit of this popular comedian of Munich.

> Mon, Tue, Fri, Sat 11.01 a.m.
> - 17.29 p.m., Sun 10.01 a.m.
> - 5.29 p.m. Tel. 22 32 66

Around where nowadays the large complex of the **German Museum (Deutsches Museum)** [9] is located (see page 77) once used to cross over the Isar river the wooden bridge of Heinrich the Lion. Immediately after, on the other side of it we see the **Müllersche Volksbad** [10] (1897-1901 by C. Holzeder), the first indoor swimming pool and the "most beautiful Art Nouveau bath in Germany". At its north side the Muffathalle, once an electrical plant, today a popular cultural events hall for Munich. Just in the vicinities, where the street climbs up away from the banks of the river stand the colossal **Cultural Center Gasteig (Kulturzentrum Gasteig)** [11], this red brick building inaugurated in 1985 is still not of the

above: **Isar Gate [8]**

middle: **Müllersches Volksbad [10]**

liking of the people of Munich, nevertheless the diversity of cultural events offered (concerts, lectures, theater plays, exhibitions, public library, adult evening classes, etc) excuse the architecture.

Cultural Center Gasteig [11] ⊃

Gasteig [11], Philharmonie ⊃

Between the Tal and the Maximilianstreet, you can find one of the "compulsory" touristic attractions, the **Hofbräuhaus am Platzl** [12].

In order to find it just follow the flow of tourists. The Hofbräuhaus is neither the oldest brewery, nor the largest, but certainly the best well know beer hall and an institution of the city. In its rooms at least 10 000 liters of beer per day are poured out in beer mugs, mostly in the garden

Hofbräuhaus [12]

Hofbräuhaus [12], Beer Garden

and in the main hall downstairs the "Schwemme". Around this place you can find other establishments, international or traditional.

We continue our stroll along the Burgstreet, by one of the oldest residential houses of Munich, the Weinstadl, into the **Alter Hof** [13]. This is the oldest fortified castle of the bavarian Dukes of the Wittelsbach dinasty, going back to 1250 and erected to defend them from the enemy and the citizens of the northeast side of the Munich of those days.

This was, between 1328 - 47, the former seat of the Emperor Ludwig the Bavarian. From the original fortress only the south-

seat of the Bavarian Ministry for the Protection of Memorials.

Opposite the imposing building of the National Theater we come out into the **Maximilianstrasse**, this is the most elegant shopping mile of Munich with famous designer shops like Gucci, Hermes, Bulgari and others that can keep up with what is good and, above all,with what is expensive.

Münzhof [14]

west Turret is to be seen, and the (reconstructed) corner watch towers. Today no traffic is allowed through here what helps to "feel" the old Munich, despite the road construction going on.

Before reaching the Maximilian-street, let´s take a look in the **Münzhof** [14] at the Hofgraben, to admire one of the oldest and most beautiful Renaissance arcaded courtyard in Germany.

From 1809 till 1983 this building served as mint house, today the

The impressive architectonical ensemble of the street is to be thanked to the King Maximilian II. It was after his ideas that in 1852 this buildings were erected with a mixture of styles, northern Neo-gothic and Italian Neo-renaissance.

National Theater

Excursion: Maximilianstreet
Well worth the walk, the Maximilianstreet towards its end, direction the Altstadtring. Pas-

Maximilianstreet

sing by the exclusive hotel Vier Jahreszeiten, opposite an interesting building in Art Nouveau style belonging to the Münchner Kammerspiele, attractive locals (Marstall), fashionable cafés (Roma) and Bars (Schumann's), and, last but not least, by the boutique of the very eccentric king of tailors Moshammer.

On the other side of the Altstadtring we find a couple of buildings in "Maximilian Style", the Ethnological Museum (Völkerkundemuseum) [126], the Upper Bavaria Government building and the statue dedicated to Max II (1875). In the green areas between both buildings the statues of Friedrich Schelling and Joseph Fraunhofer.

Marking the end of this impressive street, at the other bank of the Isar, we find the **Maximilianeum** [15] – buit in 1857-74 by Friedrich Bürklein – today seat of the Bavarian State Parliament and Senate.

Monument to Max II

**Square Max-Joseph-Platz [16]
and Memorial**

Ethnological Museum [126]

Café Roma

At the very beginnig of the Maximilianstreet we find the **Max Joseph-Platz** [16], encircled by important buildings. At the very east end the impressive complex of the Bavarian State Theatre. To the right wing the

Opera (Staatsoper) [17], inagurated in 1818, burned down in 1823; Leo von Klenze reconstructed it and in two years time opened its doors, destroyed again in the Second World War,

Hotel Vier Jahreszeiten

Maximilianeum [15]

it was rebuilt in its original form and reopened in 1963. The façade in Classical style, with the retro columns atrium and two gables – in the lower statues representing Apollo and the nine Muses, the upper with the glass mosaic shows Pegasus and the Godesses – is the perfect background for festivities.

The fine High Society of Munich enjoys during the opera season not only the performances of Haendel, Verdi, Wagner or Strauss, but as well their own "representations". Already the

King Ludwig II enjoyed here private performances of "Tristan" and other works of his idol Richard Wagner.

On the left hand of the Opera, in an empty space left by the war, that is why it seems squeezed, we find the New Residence Theater (Bayerisches Staatsschauspiel).

Opera house [17]

The Residence [18]

Dominating the north side of the square the classical-style **King's building (Königsbau)**, the Residence.The building goes back to 1826-35 when the King Ludwig I commissioned the royal architect Leo von Klenze a new seat for him and his wife with the example of the Florentine Palaces Pitti and Rucellai. The King's Building being the earliest construction of the whole complex of the Residence transformed itself, as the centuries pass by, following the necessities and the fashion of the times. (Here you can find the entrance to the

Residence [18]

Residence [18],
King's building fassade

Museum of the Residence and the Treasury, see page 21). Everything began in 1385 with the construction of a new fortified castle, the Neuveste, that the Wittelsbach let construct in the northeast of the city of those days, today only some foundations are kept.

The oldest part of the building to be seen nowadays is the fantastic **Antiquarium**, built in 1569-71 under the reign of Albrecht V. Its

almost 70 m long main Hall with a remarkable ornamented barrel vault shows so elegant and festive, thanks to the seventeen windows that allow light in, that the rulers of the State of Bavaria still use it today in occasion of special celebrations. The successor of Albrech, the Elector Wilhelm V added in 1580 the Grotto Court (Grottenhof) and the Perseus Fountain (Perseusbrunnen).

↺ *Residence [18], Vault*

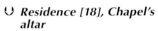
⌒ *Residence [18], Antiquarium*

↺ *Residence [18], Chapel's altar*

During the first two hundred years of the 17th century the Duke Maximilian I took care of the enlargement of the Residence and its present layout, incorporating for example the Fountain Court (Brunnenhof) at the Residencestreet, the Rich Chapel (Reiche Kapelle), the fourwinged building around the Emperor's Court (Kaiserhof) with the Imperial Staircase (Kaisertreppe), as well as the Imperial Garden (Hofgarten).

A jewel of the 18th century is the **Cuivilliés-Theater (Alte Residenztheater)**, an unique Rococo theater that the Flemish architect François Cuvilliès designed for the Elector Max III Joseph (1751-55). In the "most beautiful Rococo Theater in the world" conducted Mozart the premiere of his opera "Idomeneo"; by the way, the composer had no success in Munich.

The Theater was destroyed during the war, but its decoration could be saved in time, so nowadays the reconstruction has managed to restore it to its former glory within the Residence; its original place was where now the New Residence Theater (next to the National Theater) stands.

The **Residence** [18] the **Treasury** and the **Cuivilliès-Theater (Residenzmuseum)** can be visited with or without a guide. There is a morning guided tour showing the Ancestors Gallery, the Antiquarium, the Black Room, the Emperor's Room, the Trier Room, the Rich Room, and the Nibelung Rooms; the afternoon guided tour shows the Courts Chapel, the Parament Room, the Relics Room, the Rich Chapel, the Rich Room, the Silver Room,

Fountain Court

the Emperors Room and the Nibelung Rooms. Independently the **Treasury (Schatzkammer)** shows the precious and rare objects that the Wittelsbach since the 16th century collected: worked gold articles along with enamel, crystal, ivory work spanning ten centuries, particulary outstanding exhibits include the Cross of Queen Gisela (1006), a statuette of St. George (1599), and the crown of the king of Bavaria (1806).

Opening times: Daily 9 a.m. - 6 p.m., Thu till 8 p.m.; morning tour till 1.30 p.m., Thu till 2.30 p.m., afternoon tour from 1.30p.m., Thu from 2.30 p.m. Treasury daily 9 a.m.- 6 p.m., Thu till 8 p.m. Cuvilliès-Theater summer season daily 9 a.m. - 6 p.m., winter season till 4 p.m. (Times might change due to rehearsals and performances) Entrance Max-Joseph Platz 3. U-Bahn Odeonsplatz, Trolley 19. Tel. 29 06 71.

Residence [18], Treasury

Residence [18], Crown of the king

Residence [18], Niebelung Room

Opposite the King's building the monumental façade of the former **Main Post Office (Haupt-post)** with an open columned hall and frescoes of horses in red background, designed by Klenze in 1835, based on Florentine models. The only side of the square not royal but burgoise are the Business houses on the west side. In the middle of the square, in an imperial pose on the throne, the first king of Bavaria "to the grace of Napoleon". The **monument to Max-Josephs** is the product of the teamwork of Leo von Klenze, the sculptor of Berlin Christian Rauch and the smith Stiglmaier.

Turning into the Residenzstreet, walking along the reconstructed Renaissance façade of the Maximilian Residence (built 1611-1619) we reach the square Odeonsplatz [19] and the General's Hall.

In your way you can have a look through the triumphal entrances (in between the charming Madonna **Patrona Boiariae** by Hans Krumpper, 1616) into the Chapel Court, and further beyond the Fountain Court with the Wittelsbach Fountain [30] by Hubert Gerhart, and into the Emperor's Court.

Main Post Office

Residence [18]

The narrow, and a little dark Residenzstreet ends in a monumental architectonic ensemble, representative of the southern glamour of Munich and the Imperial power.

Responsible for this two qualities of the city is Ludwig I, who in this **Odeonsplatz** [19] with great pride spoke: "I will make out of Munich such a city, that nobody can say has seen Germany if he has not seen Munich...",

The Odeonsplatz [19], in which we are now, is surrounded by great, beautiful and impressive buildings. Direction north opens to the Ludwigstreet (that we will discover with another stroll (see page 53), towards the south closes with the General's Hall **(Feldherrnhalle)** modeled on the Loggia die Lanzi in Florence and work of Friedrich von Gärtner in 1841-44.

This is a memorial to two Bavarian generals: the Count Tilly, who in the 30 Years War commanded Bavarian Troops, and the Prince Wrede, who fought during the liberation War in 1814 against Napoleon ("The one a general, but not Bavarian, the other Bavarian but not a general" makes fun of it the Folks). In German the "Beer Hall Putsch" of the 9th of November 1923, with which Hitler entered into History, is known as the "March into the General's Hall".

General's Hall [19]

Hofgarten [20]

On the right side, where the Hall of Festivities on the north extension of the Residence [18] with the addition of the Hercules Hall forms a Concert Room of 250 meters length, opens up the Court Garden (Hofgarten) [20], it was laid out according to the principles of Italian Baroque garden design during the reign of The Elector Maximilian I at the beginning of the 17th century. The central point of this garden is the octagonal **Pavilion**, surmounted by an elegant statue of Bavaria by Hubert Gerhart (1594). The west and north of the park is surrounded by arcades; the frescoes work of Wilhelm von Kaulbach at both sides of the entrances display scenes of the History of Bavaria. To the east of the Hofgarten is the **Bavarian State Chancellery (Staatskanzlei)** [21] (1993), which dome is the restored former Museum of Bavarian army and protects the garden from the noise of the traffic of the Altstadtring.

The "prominence-seeker" Minister President Franz-Joseph-Strauß would have liked "his" palace much larger, but he encountered the opposition of the Munich Folk. In front of the building the Memorial to the War (1926), as remembrance to the fallen in both World Wars.

View from the Pavilion to the Theatiner church [22]

State Chancellery [21]

Situated to the west of the General's Hall (Feldherrnhalle) [19] the **Theatinerkirche St. Kajetan** [22], was the first church in Baroque style, north of the Alps, after the 30 Years War. The model for it was the home church of the Theatine order, S. Andrea della Valle in Rome.

Several architects worked at this construction (1663-92) Agostino Barelli, Enrico Zuccalli, Nicolo Spinelli, this last one is responsible of the towers and the cupola, which confere the building its serene character.

The first provisional façade was finished in 1765-68 in Rococo style by François Cuvillies. The building was a gift of Elector Ferdinand Maria and his wife Henriette Adelaide in gratitude for the birth of their long-awaited heir Max Emanuel

(1662). The interior is laid out according to Roman models. The crypt contains the sarcophagus of the sponsoring couple, Max Emanuel and several Electors and Kings members of the Wittelsbach dinasty.

Theatiner church [22]

Theatiner church [22]

Leaving the Odeonsplatz [19] and turning into the elegant shopping street Brienner Strasse we arrive to the beautiful (thanks to the harmonious proportions) **Wittelsbacher Platz** [23], (in the middle of the square the equestrian statue of the Elector Maximilian I by Berthel Thorwaldsen, 1839).

If we turn again to the left we leave the street, but if we follow straight with the sight we reach to see the **Obelisk** [24] at the Karolinenplatz; designed by Leo von Klenze (1833), is a monument to the 30 000 Bavarian soldiers who died on the battle field or frozen during Napoleon's Russian campaign.

Behind the Karolinenplatz we find the Museums quarter, with the inauguration of the Pinakothek der Moderne [25] (2002)

has turned into the most important and concentrated center for Museums in Europe. (see page 52).

Obelisk [24]

*Wittelsbach Square and
equestrian statue [23]*

As we continue we come into the **Amiraplatz**, followed by the **Salvatorplatz** [26] we cannot call them really squares, but wide streets. In here three Cultural Institutions have their seat: to the left the Bavarian Culture Ministry (using one wing of the former Theatiner Monastery destroyed mostly in 1944), next to it the headquarters of the Bookshop Hugendubel, and opposite the **Literaturhaus**, center of the literary life of the city (with the Café-Restaurant Dukatz, visited also by not so literary Münchners). Next to it the unobtrusive **church Salvatorkirche**, a brick construction in the style of the late Gothic, erected in 1494 as cemetery church for the cathedral church of "our lady" and since 1829 home of the Greek-orthodox community in Munich.

*Literaturhaus and the church
Salvatorkirche [26]* ⊃

The **Salvatorplatz** [26] leads into the Kardinal-Faulhaber-Street, where the Archbishop of Munich-Freising has his residence,

as the chiefs of the Bavarian Banks, but we do not want to draw conclusions. Here and there we can feel the Feudal atmosphere of the former nobility homes.

The Archbishop's Palace (Erzbischöfliche Palais) [27] (Kardinal-Faulhaber-Street 7) has the oldest Rococo façade in the city, constructed in 1733-37 by François Cuvilliès and J. B. Zimmermann for the Duke Holstein. The house number 2 is the Palace Porcia, built in 1693 by Enrico Zuccalli for the Duke Fugger, later pur-

Archbishop's Palace [27]

chased by the Elector Karl Albrecht for his mistress, the later Princess Porcia, and redecorated by François Cuvilliès in Rococo style. We can have a look in the **Prannerstreet** leading to Maximilian square, there we find the palace Neuhaus-Preysing-Palais (Nr. 2, beautiful Rococo façade), the palace Seinsheim (Nr. 7) and the palace Gise (Nr. 9, both with remarkable Rococo façade).

Still in the Kardinal Faulhaber Street, but transported to the present we can have a look to the **Fünf Höfe**, the now a days most fashionable shopping paradise in Munich for people with high pretensions and thick purse. We find here as well the Entrance to the Cultural foundation **Kunsthalle der Hypo-Kulturstiftung** [28], which art exhibitions are well worth seeing. (Theatinerstreet 8).

> ℹ Daily 10 a.m. - 8 p.m.
> Tel. 22 42 12.

Fünf Höfe [28]

Back into the Kardinal-Faul-haber-Street we end into the square **Promenadeplatz**, at its corner (Nr. 2) stands the **Palace Montgelas**, a palace in the classical style with partially the original decoration, today integrated in the luxurious hotel Bayerischer Hof.

Strolling around the Promenadeplatz, lovely with the little gardens, we can catch a glimpse of the **Gunetzrhainerhaus** with the lovely Rococo façade (Promenadeplatz 15) and above all of the **Church of the Holy Trinity (Dreifaltigkeitskirche)** [29] (Pacellistrasse 6).

The late Baroque façade based on plans of Antonio Viscardi in 1711-18 has a convex form and is the first of this type to be build in Munich. Inside, the dome frescoe The Holy Trinity in Heaven by C. D. Asam is one of the most important in Munich.

Continuing in the same direction we arrive to the generously laid square Lenbachplatz [30] containing the probably most

beautiful fountain of Munich, the **Wittelsbach Fountain** by Adolf von Hildebrand (1893-95).

The opposite forces of water are symbolized here: the woman on an bull the positive effects, the struggling man on a horseback the destructive ones.

Church of the Holy Trinity [29]

Bayerischer Hof

Between the Promenadeplatz and the Maffeistreet a pedestrian passage leads to the largest historic construction in the city and the best-known landmark, the Cathedral Church of Our Lady **(Dom Zu Unserer Lieben Frau)**, also known as the **Frauenkirche** [31]. The foundation stone was laid in 1468 by Duke Sigismund, Jörg von Halsbach was commissioned to build it, in 1488 the towers of about 98,50 Meters were finished, in 1494 the church was ceremoniously consecrated, in 1525 the towers became the characteristic "onion domes". They are precursors of the Renaissance and with the roof of the building unmistakable from the distance.

Wittelsbacher Brunnen [30]

Frauenkirche [31] – Cathedral Church of Our Lady

The cathedral is indeed massive: 109 m length, 41,5 m wide; its interior was designed to hold a congregation of 20 000, despite the fact that, at the time, Munich had only 13 000 inhabitants. Nevertheless does not seem to be oversized, as the three naves are very harmoniously divided by eleven pairs of pillars.

The irregular polygonal Choir keeps totally to the tradition of southern German Wide-span-churches. After the reconstruction works in 1994 the numerous objects of art of the interior have made their way back.

Among others the **Choir Windows**, partly belonging to the previous building, the first of all depicting the Annunciation (1392); the **Statues of Apostles and Prophets of the Choir stool** by Erasmus Grasser (1502), the gilded bass-reliefs with scenes of the **Life of Mary** by Ignaz Günther (1744), in the choir stool too; **The Cenotaph for the Emperor Ludwig the Bavarian**, 1620 by Hans Krumpper ordered by the Elector Maximilian.

Remarkable as well the Ascension of the Virgin by Peter Candid (1620) above the sacristy door, the Virgin of the cloak by Jan Pollack (about 1500) and a Madonna by Hans Leinberger to the right of the entrance of the choir (1520).

Behind the choir a staircase leads to the **Crypt**, there rest the bodies of the Wittelsbach rulers, and the one of the last Bavarian King Ludwig III. In another tomb lay the Archbishops of Munich-Freising since 1825. The **climbing** of the 98 meters high South tower is worth the effort, despite the narrow staircase.

Frauenkirche [31] – Cathedral Church of Our Lady

Fishing Museum (Jagd- und Fischereimuseum) [32] (Neuhauser Strasse 2); over 500 stuffed animals, hunting weapons and equipment, and plenty more to make threir heart beat.

April till October Mon. to Sat. 10 a.m. - 5 p.m. Sun and holidays closed.

Frauenkirche [31], Cenotaph

In the south side of the square Frauenplatz two narrow lanes lead to the **Pedestrian area**, the Kaufinger Strasse, which name has nothing to do with "shopping" but refers to an old noble family of Munich.

If you turn to the left, a couple of steps takes you back to the starting point of this stroll, the Marienplatz [1]. We turn to the right, direction the Karlsplatz (Stachus) [37], where the main commercial and pedestrian area finishes at the Karlstor [36].

Hunters and Fishermen should not pass by the **Hunting and**

Daily 9.30 a.m. - 5 p.m., Mon, Thu 9.30 a.m. - 9 p.m. Neuhauser Strasse 2. S-, U-Bahn Marienplatz. Telephone 22 05 22

Hunting and Fishing Museum [32]

Neuhauser Street

☾ *Hunting and Fishing Museum [32]*

The most important building in this street is the **Church of St Michael (Michaelskirche)** [33], constructed in 1583-97 by the architect Friedrich Sustris for the Jesuit Order and sponsored by the Duke Michael V. In the wake of the Counter Reformation, to prove his nick-name "the Pious", the building costs almost drove the state into bankruptcy.

The barrel vault with a diameter of 20 m was, after the one in St Peter in Rome, the second largest in the Christian world. It is a pity that the majority passes by without paying attention to the magnificent façade which represent both authorities, the earthy and the holy. The entrance is presided by a bronze statue of the Archangel Michael doing battle with the evils of the world (by Hubert Gerhart, 1592). Above the niches contain the ancestors from which the Dukes claim their rank and honor: Agilolfing, Karoling, Wittelsbach.

St. Michael fighting the Devil
[33]

Church of St. Michael [33]
and the Old Academy

In the interior the dominant figure are the strong and big pillars on top of which the weight of the Barrel vault relies. Everything has a subliminal meaning: The triumphal arch of the Cancel, which divides the choir and its dominating High Altar (Painting of the St. Michael fighting the Devil by Christoph Schwarz, 1587) from the transepts means to symbolize the victory of the Counter Reformation. The Crypt beneath the chancel is the burial place of the Duke Wilhelm V, the Elector Maximilian I and the King Ludwig II.

Bürgersaal church [35]

The west end of the façade is part of the Jesuit College of those days, later this building housed the Academy of Fine Arts and the **Old Academy (Alte Akademie)** [34] of the University. Today contains the headquarters of the Regional Statistics Office. Further along we find the discrete **Bürgersaal church** [35] (Neuhauser Strasse 47), assembly hall for men of the Marian confraternity of 1709-10. The most precious decoration is the Guardian Angel group by Ignaz Günther (1763) located under the organ console. The crypt contains the tomb of the Jesuit Father Rupert Mayer, whose opposition to the Nazis cost him his life. (+ 1945, sanctified by Pope Johannes Paul in 1987).

A few steps still to the **Karl's Gate (Karlstor)** [36]; as the Isar Gate [8] and the Sendlinger Gate [41] part of the second city fortifications of the 14th century erected by Ludwig the Bavarian. Since then has suffered multiple transformations, but still keeps its essential dividing character between "in" and "out". Through the gate we reach the square **Karlsplatz** [37], also called **Stachus** in honor of a popular inn named Zum Eustachus.

Opposite the square stand imposing the neo-Renaissance building of the **Palace of Justice (Justizpalast)** with a monumental dome which created polemic at the time of construction (1887-97 by Friedrich von Thiersch).

View to Karl's gate [36]

Palace of Justice by Stachus [37]

Stachus fountain [37]

Turning to the left we get in to the Sonnenstreet, which follows the line of the once standing city walls, and we turn immediately again to the left in to the Herzogspitalstreet. Passing by the oldest wine bar of Munich, Weinhaus Neuner, we reach at the corner of the crossing with the Damenstiftstreet the late Baroque **Collegiate Church of St. Anne (Damenstiftskirche St. Anna)** [38], built by J. B. Gunetzrhainer in 1732. The interior (stucco and frescoes) are work of the brothers Asam.

This church suffered the same fate during the war as the others in the historical center, only some years later could be rebuilt with care. Next to the church stretches the building that once homed the convent of the sisters of the Salesian order. Opposite, work as well of Gunetzrhainer, the **Palace Lerchenfeld-Palais** [39], with a lovely Rococo façade.

The crossing formed by the Altheimer Eck, Brunn- and Hackenstreet belongs to one of the oldest quarters in town and invites to a stroll. At the corner of the Hacken- Hotterstreet stands the probably eldest restaurant of Munich, the Hundskugel. Opposite one of the most charming addresses in town, the Radspielerhouse (Hackenstrasse 7), built in 1678 as link between two old houses.

Hier lived Heinrich Heine from November 1827 to July 1828; he applied (unsuccessfully) for a chair in Literature at the University of Munich. Behind this house, where now you can find decoration stuff and presents, almost hiding, a bucolic garden with fountain and trees, a luxury that the private owners enjoy, hopefully, for a long time !

Radspielerhouse

Hundskugel

The courtyard Asamhof with its beautiful shops and establishment opens up to the Sendlinger Street, this was once the route towards the south, here the trade direction Tirol and Italy found its way. Here as well, discreet, integrated in the façade of the old and new residential houses, and overseen by inexpert eyes, the most beautiful Temple of God of Munich, the **Church of St. Johann-Nepomuk** [40], named as well **Asamkirche**. The architectonic jewel, just 9 m wide and 30 m long, is a complete work of the brothers Egid Quirin and Cosmas Damian Asam, who did not only designed, built, decorated and ornamented it, but as well, and against the will of the folk, imposed themselves and, last but not least, financed it (1733-46). "A masterpiece of late Baroque interior decoration showing the joy of living, threshold of Rococo", praise the Art historians. The façade with the soft colors represents the life and death of St. Johann Nepomuk, who was sanctified just a few years before. The two stored highly ornamented interior was meant to inspire a mystical feeling; though one could feel in a fantastic theater room prepared for a magnificent show, specially in the morning when the rays of the sun strike, through an oval window, the High altar.

The Asam house (1733) and the vica-rage house (1771) flank the church on both sides. At the end of the street we find the already mentioned Sendlinger gate [41], beyond it can be seen the Protestant church of Saint Mathew (1953/55 by Gustav Gsaenger).

Sendlinger Gate [41]

Asamkirche [40]

Church Asamkirche [40]

Walking along the Sendlinger Street we come back to the Marienplatz [1], where we finish our stroll along the Historical center. Parallel to it we find the **City Museum (Stadtmuseum)** with the various collections: theater puppets, music instruments, fashion, photography and film (with interesting historical films).

Amid the permanent collections specially interesting: Stadtbild München (Models of the city along five centuries); the Moris-kensaal (with the Maruska dancers of Erasmus Grasser, 1480) and the Munich home decor, with emphasis on the period between 1888 and 1910.

> **i** Daily 10 a.m. - 6 p.m., Mon closed.
> Sankt-Jakobs-Platz 1. U- and S-Bahn Marienplatz.
> Tel. Operator 233-22 370, Program 233 25 586.

City Museum

City Museum, Maruska dancer

Through the Museums Quarter

We begin our tour in the circular shaped square **Karolinenplatz** [24]; the obelisk in the middle, by Leo von Klenze (1833), reminds of a tragic passage of history, when 30 000 Bavarian soldiers lost their lives in the campaigns against Napoleon in 1812.

From here and direction to the city center the Brienner Street leads to the square Königsplatz [A]. Before arriving here the agreement of 1938 was signed by Great Britain, France, Italy and Germany), homes the College of Music. Between both stood the Temple of Honors, today only left overs of the foundations to be seen as it was destroyed immediately after the war.

The **Königsplatz** [A], a real "royal" square, was planned by Ludwig I in 1817, when he was still the prince, and completed in 1862 when Leo von Klenze finished the Propyläen. Along with the Ludwigstreet represents

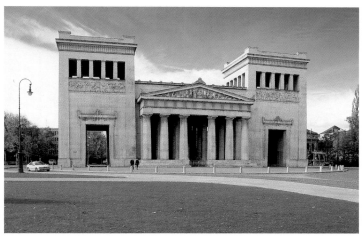

Königsplatz [A]

crossing with Meiser-/Arcisstreet holds two monumental buildings from the times of the Nazis, when Munich was the "capital of the movement". The projects are from Paul Ludwig Troost, who designed the House of the German Art too.

The building on the left, once the Headquarters of the NSDAP, homes today the Central Institute of Art History, the Building to the right, Hitler's former Conference Building (here the Munich his most monumental contribution to Munich in its present form and shows his aims to turn the city, to much the dislike of the people, into the "Athens on the Isar".

Glyptothek [A]

At the north side of the square stands the **Glyptothek** [A], erected in 1816-1830 by Leo von Klenze following the project of Carl von Fischer. The four-wings-complex in classical ionic style was constructed to contain – as it does now a days – the collection of antique sculptures. In total 160 statues.

Chronologically the tour starts with the Archaic epoch and, along the 13 rooms around the light courtyard, finishes with the sculptures and bass-relief of the High Empire times.

Its finest works include the famous Aegineten, late-archaic sculptures from the front of the Temple of Aegina, excavated in 1811, in Munich since 1827; the two Kouroi (archaic young men statues), the Mnesarete tomb relief, the Apollo by Tenea, the Barberini Faun and the bust of the Emperor Augustus.

⊂ *Glyptothek [A], Exhibits*

> ℹ Daily 10 a.m. - 5 p.m., Thu 10 a.m. - 8 p.m., Mon closed. Königsplatz 3. U-Bahn Königsplatz. Telephone 28 61 00

Glyptothek [A], Barberini Faun

Complementary to the Glyptothek [A] on the south side of the square stands the **Museum of Classical Art (Antikensammlung)**, resembling a Greek temple with the eight columns of the Corinthian order by Georg Friedrich Ziebland (1838-48).

It contains the Wittelsbach collection of Greek vases, Etruscan and Greek ceramic as well as smaller pieces of different origins (gold jewellery, terracottas, glass, silver, bronze). Worth admiration are the fantastic attic vases from the 6th and 5th century B. C. and the Greek jewels from the Classical epoch.

The **Propyläen**, which closes the west side of the square, is a purely decorative building. Inspired by the main entrance of the Athenian Acropolis should remind us of the close links between Bavaria and Greece, where Ludwig's second son, Otto, with the help of his father, was elected king in 1832.

The dynastic union was predestinated to separation. Otto had to abdicate. Nevertheless the Propyläen has survived the tempests of the passing of time.

The sculptures and relief in the front and in the towers represent scenes of the wars of independence of Greece against Turkey.

• Daily 10a.m.-5p.m., Wed.
i 10a.m.-8p.m., Mon closed.
Königsplatz 1. U-Bahn
Königsplatz. Tel. 28 61 00.

Lenbach House [A]

Beyond the Propyläen the next museum waits already for us, the **City Gallery in the Lembach House (Städtische Galerie im Lenbachhaus)** [A]. It was built in 1887 by Gabriel von Seidl for the "painter prince" Franz von Lenbach as a Noble Villa in Florentine style. Later the actual north wing would be enlarged.

The main building and the atelier houses the great State Collection of Paintings of the 19th and 20th century. A "gold mine" for the lovers of the Munich Romantic and Land-scape School (Adam, Dillis, Kobell, Spitzweg, Lenbach, Corinth)!

So important as the above mentioned are the works of the Foundation Gabriele Münter with the collections of the Blaue Reiter (Marc, Kandinsky, Macke, Jawlensky, Münter etc.) you can find works of Klee, Kubin, Josef Beuys and contemporaries.

Part of the building is the **Kunst-bau** (entrance to be found in the subway station), changing exhi-bitions inform of the latest trends and tendencies in the international art scene.

> **i** Daily 10 a.m. - 6 p.m., Mon closed. Luisenstrasse 33. U-Bahn Königsplatz. Telephone 233 320 00.

The museums quarter of Mu-nich has gained so much im-portance since the inauguration of the Pinakothek der Moderne [25] that is one of the top addresses world wide.

The Pinakothek-Trio can com-pete with Paris, London, Berlin and New York. We present the three, which are divided just by green areas and one street, in chronological order.

Alte Pinakothek [B]

The **Alte Pinakothek** [B] is one of the oldest museums in the world. The King Ludwig I, a visionary in matters of art and civil architecture, commissioned it, in order to give access to "his Folk to enjoyment and education" through the large private collections of art of the Wittelsbach family. Again the "royal architect" Leo von Klenze was commissioned this great Neo-renaissance project.

Today around 850 paintings of five centuries of European painting (14th-18th century) are contained here.

Almost all the big names of the different times and countries are represented.

The largest portion of the works on show is the collection of Old German and Dutch Masters (Michael Pachers: "The altar with the fathers of the Church", the Cologne Master, Albrecht Altdorf: "The battle of Alexander", Dürer's Selfportrait and the "Four Apostles", Lukas Cranach d. Ä.: "Christ crucifixion", Matt-

hias Grünewald: "St. Erasmus and St. Mauritius".

Great works of the Italian Renaissance Masters Leonardo da Vinci, Raffael and Tizian with the famous »Portrait of the Emperor Karl V.« and his late "Thorn crowning".

One of the most important collections of paintings by Rubens is here, but we find as well Anthonis van Dyck and Rembrandt. You can admire French works of Nicolas Poussin, Claude Lorrain, amid plenty more Boucher's Portrait of the beautiful Madame Pompadour.

Spain is represented by the serial of "rogues" of Murillo. We can only mention a few here, the not mentioned ones are well worth seeing too.

> **i** Daily 10 a.m. - 5 p.m., Thu 10 a.m. - 10 p.m., Mon closed. Barer Strasse 27, Entrance Theresienstrasse, U-Bahn Theresienstrasse; Tram 27. Tel. 238 05-216.

above: **Alte Pinakothek [B]**   **Neue Pinakothek [B]**

Opposite the **Neue Pinakothek** [B], dates back to the times of Ludwig I too. The king wanted to have a house for the works of art of his time and commissioned Friedrich von Gaertner another Pinakothek which was inaugurated in 1851 and completely destroyed in WW II. The new "postmodernist" construction of Alexander von Branca displays around 550 paintings and 50 sculptures (total records 4500 paintings, 300 sculptures) spanning an overview above all of the paintings from the end of the 18th century to the beginning of the 20th. To begin with we could mention international names like Gainsborough, Turner, Goya, David, followed by the Romantics (C. D. Friedrich, Blechen), representative of the Munich School from Rottmann through Spitzweg to Moritz von Schwind, The Nazarens and the

above: **Neue Pinakothek [B]**   **Pinakothek der Moderne [25]**

French Realists like Corot, Millet, Courbet. The modern times present themselves with the Impressionists Manet, Monet, Degas, Renoir, Pissarro reaching the peak with the trilogy Cezanne, van Gogh, Gauguin. The golden end is conform by Liebermann, Slevoigt and Corinth and representatives of the Symbolism and Modernism as Klinger, Klimt, Hodler and Toulouse-Lautrec.

Daily 10 a.m. - 5 p.m.,
Thur 10 a.m. - 10 p.m. Mon
closed. Barer Strasse 29,
Entrance Theresienstrasse
U-Bahn Theresienstraße;
Tram 27. Tel. 238 05 -195.

Daily 10 a.m. - 5 p.m.,
Thur, Fri 10 a.m. - 8 p.m.
Barer Strasse 40.
U-Bahn Theresienstrasse;
Tram 27. Tel. 238 05 -360.

In September 2002, behind sque-
dule, finally the **Pinakothek der
Moderne** [25] was inaugurated.
Even if the architect Stephan
Braunfels had to fight against
the Bavarian cultural burocracy
and the costs cuts, it has turn
out to be one of the most
successful museum projects of
our times, and even maybe the
most beautiful of all.

Pinakothek der Moderne [25]

The challenge was great: to
house four important collections of different fields art,
graphic, architecture, and design
under the same roof.

Pinakothek der Moderne [25]

The collection of art spans between the classical Modernists
(Picasso, Kandinsky, Klee, Mag-
ritte, Beckmann) through Beuys
and Warhol to the contemporaries as Pipilotti Rist, Bruce
Neumann and Olaf Metzel. The
Graphic collection shows dra-
wings and graphic prints from
Leonardo till our days in changing exhibitions.

Amalienstreet) are characteri-
zed by a vast selection of bookshops, antique shops, cafés and
pubs.

The Architecture museum and
the New Collection (with
50 000 objects of the avant-
garde art) show their treasures
in different accessible ways.

Around the Pinakothek der
Moderne [25] the streets are
getting more and more art
galleries, design shops and
similars.

The lively streets leading to the
north, direction the University
quarter (Barer Street, Türken- und

King Ludwig I

Ludwigstreet, Schwabing, English Garden, Lehel

The north of the **Odeonsplatz** [19] forms part of the brilliant entrance to the **Ludwigstreet**, together with the former concert hall Odeon (destroyed during the war, reconstructed as Finance Ministry), the palace Leuchtenberg (1816-21 by Klenze, today the Ministry of Finances) and the Bazar building opposite (1825/26 by Klenze).

It was build up by the architects Klenze and Gärtner for Ludwig I between 1920 and 1940 against the will of the Folk. It is one of the most important works of civil architecture of the century and represents with consequence the concept that Ludwig had of "his" kingdom.

Both ends of the street are underlined by the personal souvenirs of the trips of the king: the General's Hall (Feldherrnhalle) [19] remembrance of the Florentine Renaissance, and the Victory Gate (Siegestor) [102] standing for the classical Rome.

The wishes of the monarch of occupying the houses with noble families was not fulfilled, in spite of that we find Ministries and Administration offices. The atmosphere in the street is rather cool and strict and not very inviting to stroll along (no shops!), nevertheless this does not rest importance and monumentality.

Bayerische Staatsbibliothek

Other important buildings in the Ludwigstreet are: the former Ministry of War (Nr. 14, today the Bavarian City Archive), the Bavarian State Library (Bayerische Staatsbibliothek) (today almost 5 millions books, the largest in Germany), the two towered **Ludwig church** (Nr. 20) with a monumental fresco of the Last judgement by Peter Cornelius (1836-40) and the **Ludwig Maximilian University** [101], erected by Gärtner in 1835-40.

Here the street widens up in to a forum, named Geschwister-Scholl-Platz (West side) and Professor-Huber-Platz (East side) in memory of the leaders of the university opposition group the White Rose, who were executed in 1943.

In this forum the meeting point of the students are the two characteristic "roman" fountains. This university with about 45 000 students is one of the largest in Germany.

The monumental end of the street is the **Victory Gate (Siegestor)** [102]. Inspired by the Constantine Arch in Rome and topped by the Bavaria leading the Chariot of Lions was built in 1843-50. It intended to be a monument in honor of the Bavarian army who fought against Napoleon.

The new inscription on the south side was added after it was damaged during WW II: "Consecrated for victory, destroyed by war, an admonition to peace".

Ludwig Maximilian University [101]

Geschwister-Scholl-Platz [101]

The Victory Gate is the starting point of Leopoldstreet, called too Boulevard Leopold, the axis avenue of the suburb of **Schwabing** [103]. Once a village, later the meeting place of artists, it does not have the same aura as some may expect, it changed completely after the war: the right side of the street, mostly around the Wedekindplatz, all kind of entertainment and pinchbeck / rip-off establishments, and here and there a couple of real pearls like the theater Lustspielhaus (Occamstreet 8) and the Lach- und Schiessgesellschaft (Haimhauser- / corner with Ursulastreet).

The left side of the Leopoldstreet is dominated by a lively residential area with old apartments for Professors, Journalists, Artists with a name, and several

Victory Gate [102]

bookshops (e. g. Lehmkuhl), boutiques, art shops, restaurants.

The Leopoldstreet itself with the street terraces and ice-cream-places is a popular stroll avenue, the sidewalks are the catwalk of the latest makes of Porsche or Landrover.

The only "sight" is to be found in the building of the insurance company Münchner Rückversicherung, with an exhibition room for artists with good connections, in front of the building the 17 meters high figure "The Walking Man" by Borowsky (1995).

Street café

The Walking Man

⊂ *Monopteros [C]*

Revolution!), later on, in 1804, the garden architect Ludwig von Sckell enlarged it. The north part, beyond the street Mittlere Ring, is wider and bigger but not so popular as the south part with its attractions.

We recommend a tour: beginning at the lake Kleinhesseloher See with swans, paddle and row boats, restaurant and beer garden; then around the lake and following the paths along the creek Eisbach, to the Chinese Tower (Chinesischen Turm), a restaurant with beer garden, horse carriages and an old fashioned children merry-go-round.

If you want to reach the **English Garden** [C] you can turn by the Universtity in to the Veterinär-street or, if you would like to soak in to the atmosphere of the "Boulevard-Leopold", afterwards in to the Martiusstreet. The favorite park of the Munchners is for sure the English Garden, about 5 km. long and around 1 km wide, functions as the precious green lung of the metropolis and is one of the largest green areas within the city in Europe.

On the suggestion of the Count Rumford, the Prince Elector Karl Theodor had this garden laid in 1789 (the year of the French

Walking further we come upon the Monopteros, a classical style temple on top of a hill, offering a great view over the city skyline. The last stage, again along the creek, reaches the Japanese Tea House, a present of Japan to the city of Munich on the occasion of the Olympic Games of 1972, and ends up in the Prinzregentstreet at the Haus der Kunst [104]. Duration of the tour between 1 1/2 and 3 hours.

Lake Kleinhesseloher See [C]

Chinese Tower [C]

English Garden [C]

English Garden [C]

The **Prinzregentenstreet**, with the Ludwig- and Maximilian-street, is the last of the three monumental avenues laid in the 19th century (from 1891 onwards). Begins with the classicist Prinz-Karl-Palace (1804-06 by Karl Fischer), skirts the south end of the English Gardens and continues by the Haus der Kunst, over the bridge Prinz-regentenbrücke to the other side of the Isar where finishes at Bogenhausen with the Prinz-regentenplatz square.

The Haus der Kunst [104], planned by Paul Ludwig Troost and completed in 1937 was inaugurated as "House of German Art", and is a perfect example of monumental architecture of the Nazi time. It was used as exhibition room of the yearly shows of the "third reich". After 1945 served different purposes, for example housing the Staats-galerie Moderne Kunst, whose works are now exhibited in the Pinakothek der Moderne [25] (see page 52). The central and east wing of the building are in use for changing exhibitions of excellent reputation thanks to the work of the long time mana-ging director Christoph Vitali.

> **i** Daily 10 a.m. - 10 p.m.
> Prinzregentenstreet 1.
> U-Bahn Odeonsplatz;
> Bus 53. Telephone 211 27-0.

Prinz-Karl-Palace

Haus der Kunst [104]

Bavarian National Museum [105]

The first building erected in the Prinzregentenstreet was the **Bavarian National Museum (Bayerische Nationalmuseum)** [105] (1894-99 by Gabriel v. Seidl). Gathers all the styles typical of the Historical one but conforms a unity such that represents perfectly the taste at that time. Works at the same time as Art and History of civilization museum and contains treasures that, neither the locals, nor the tourist, know to appreciate in its real worth. That is due to the fact that the collections are not presented in a clear way, nevertheless since some time an effort has been made to correct this.

In front of the east wing the equestrian statue of the Prince Luitpold by Adolf von Hildebrand. The main and upper floors contain the collection of the History of civilization with an overview on the epochs from the early Middle Ages to the Jugendstil. With main emphasis on late Gothic paintings and sculptures (sculptures by Riemenschneider, Grasser, Leinberger) and the Bavarian Baroque and Rococo (Ignaz Günther-Saal).

But we find as well bronze and ivory sculptures, glass paintings, Flemish tapestries, Italian Majolica, ivory, Meissen and Nymphenburg porcelaine.

Bavarian National Museum [105]

The collection of Folkloric Crafts comprises among others farmer's rooms, pottery, farming tools, games, clocks and measuring instruments.

The world well known collection of cribs with over 60 000 figurines from Tirol, Naples and Sicily is unique in the world and attracts visitors not only at Christmas time.

Daily 10 a.m. - 5 p.m., Thu 10 a.m. - 8 p.m., Mon closed. Prinzregentenstr. 3. U-Bahn Lehel; Tram 17; Bus 53. Tel. 211 24-01.

Bavarian National Museum [105]

Bavarian National Museum [105], Silver-ware of the Prince Bishop of Hildesheim

∩ Bavarian National Museum [105], Crib figurine

⊂ Bavarian National Museum [105], Judith with the head of Holofernes

∪ Bavarian National Museum [105], Room with exhibits

⊂ *Bavarian National Museum [105]*

The Prinzregentenstreet crosses over the Isar and transforms in a terrace derived from Florentine garden design, culminating in the **Angel of Peace (Friedensengel)** [107]. The architectonical and sculptural group was a donation to commemorate the 25th anniversary of the Peace of Versailles (1871).

The group is composed by three parts: a small open hall with relief sculptures of German emperors and mosaic medals (symbols of War and Peace), a 23 meters high Corinthian column, and the Angel of peace itself, a winged golden figure corresponding to the Nike of Olympia, who holds a palm branch in the right hand and a figure of Pallas Athena in the left.

Beyond the Oettingenstreet we come upon a former noble palace, the **Schackgalerie** [106], the count Schack acquired a remarkable collection of works by German painters of the 19th century. The lovers of Moritz v. Schwind (31 Main works), Arnold Böcklin (16), Anselm Feuerbach (11) should not miss the visit.

You can admire here Rottmann, Spitzweg, Schleich d. Ä., Lenbach and others too.

i	Daily 10 a.m. - 5 p.m., Mon closed. Prinzregentenstreet 9. Bus 53. Tel. 238 05 - 224.

The Angel of Peace [107]

On the right side of the street, behind the Angel of Peace, in the "upper classes" quarter of Bogenhousen, we find the remarkable Neo-classical palace **Villa Stuck** [108]. Franz von Stuck, so called (as Lenbach) the "painter prince", designed for his own in 1898 this complete work of art with studio accordingly to his particular taste, in order to celebrate his memorable artists' parties.

The unique combination of Clas-

of the 19th and 20th century.

> **i** Daily 10 a.m. - 6 p.m., Mon closed. Prinzregentenstr. 60. U-Bahn Prinzregentenplatz; Bus 53. Tel. 45 55 51 25.

*Villa Stuck [108],
Studio 1914/15, View from the
Prinzregentenstreet*

sical forms, symbolic themes, and antique-like decoration provokes in the visitors a cool reaction.

The villa is the Center of Art Nouveau Research in Munich. The changing exhibitions concentrate in the art of the turning

The Prinzregentenstreet turns into the square Prinzregentenplatz, dominated by the **Prinzregenten Theater** [109]. Built in 1900-01 as Opera house, damaged badly during the war, it is only in the 80'/90' that could be used again as concert room due to its fantastic acustic.

Prinzregenten Theater [109]

Worth to have a look to is the beautiful Gartensaal, though only to be seen during performances.

> **i** Prinzregentenplatz 12. U-Bahn Prinzregentenplatz; Bus 53. Tel. 2185-2959.

Prinzregenten Theater [109]

The sporting north of Munich –
Between the Olympic Center and the Allianz Stadium

The north part of the city gained in attractive thanks to the 20th Summer Olympic Games. The **Olympia Park** [110], built from 1968 after the plans of the architects Behnisch and partners, was laid out on the grounds of the former first airport of Munich. It turned to be the most beautiful sport park one could imagine to the pleasure of the people in Munich.

buildings: the **Olympic Stadium**, the Olympic Hall and the Olympic Swimming Pool with the legendary net-like roof, which set new standards for the architecture of the century. The daring construction of the acrylic-tiled-roof is held by 12 big Pillars 81 meters high and 36 smaller ones.

Added to these we find the Olympic Ice Stadium with an open air skating ground, and the

Olympia Park [110]

be the most beautiful sport park one could imagine to the pleasure of the people in Munich.

The highlights of this almost 3 square-kilometers area are the 52-meter-hill, the with alpine vegetation covered Olympia-berg, made of rubbles of the bombed city; an artificial lake, fed by the Nymphenburger canal and the group of sport

Small Olympic Hall, the former Bicycle Race Stadium. Everything "peered down" by the 289 m. height **Olympic Tower (Olympia- und Fernsehturm)**. Two elevators bring the visitors, with a speed of 7 m/sec, up to two platforms of 189 and 192 meters altitude. On a clear day the view reaches from Dachstein to Säntis, an alpine panorama spanning 400 km! In the restaurant below you can combine sitting down both, the enjoyment of the view, with eating and drinking, as the revolving platform provides a complete bird's eye-view of the city every hour or so.

> **i** Olympia Park open to the public. Olympic Stadium daily 8.30 a.m. - 6 p.m., winter time 9 a.m. - 4.30 p.m. – Olympic Tower daily 9 a.m. - 12 p.m. (last ascention 11.30 p.m. restaurant from 11 a.m.). Visitors "Info-Pavillon" at the Eissportzentrum. U-Bahn Olympiazentrum; several Bus lines. Telephone 30 67- 24 14.

BMW-Hochhaus with the BMW Museum [111]

> **i** Daily 9 a.m. - 5 p.m. Petuelring 130. U-Bahn Olympiazentrum; several Bus lines. Telephone 38 22-33 07.

Walking distance from the Olympic grounds is the **BMW-Hochhaus** and the **BMW Museum** [111]. The unusual architectural construction with the form of four cylinders grouped around an open shaft (design Karl Schwanzer, 1970-73) are the headquarters of the administration of BMW.

In contrast to it the windowless, silver-colored concrete bowl houses the Museum. The exhibition Zeithorizonte traces the major developments in the history of BMW stretching back almost 80 years.

Which is the development of the values of work, factory, electronics, environment, free time and which is the role that the human being plays in it? With help of visual technologies such as 100 films, videos and slides cast light on developments and visions.

Further away in the north, in the suburb of Fröttmaning, still in construction, the polemic **Allianz-Arena** [112], the football stadium where the opening game of the World Championship of 2006 should take place.

66 000 covered seats, 2000 business seats, 100 tribunes will cost 280 mill. Euros, added to them 185 millions should go for the infrastructure like accesses, public transportation etc.

It is not a surprise to know that not all the people are fascinated by it, taking into account that the budget will be exceeded. The positive part is the futuristic design "Swimming belt" of the Architect Team Herzog-de Meuron with their changing lights effect. Who would like to visit

the building site must just hold
tight to the cranes!

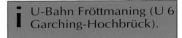

i U-Bahn Fröttmaning (U 6
Garching-Hochbrück).

above:
Allianz-Arena

bottom:
Nymphenburg Castle [113]

Nymphenburg Castle and Park [113]

In the year 1663, overjoyed by the birth of his son and heir, the Elector Ferdinand Maria offered his wife Adelaide a piece of ground in the very far west of the Residence [18].

In the following years would be built here a villa in Italian style, the central section first, then the Elector Max Emanuel, the long-time-awaited son, added a gallery and the side wings.

The first works of this place are the efforts of Agostino Barelli, from 1673 of Enrico Zuccalli and from 1714 onwards, after the return from the exile in Holland of Max Emanuel, of Joseph Effner. This one gave the final touch to the Castle and built the Pagodenburg, the Badenburg and the Hermitage of Mary Magdalena.

Max Emanuel´s sucessor, Karl Albrecht, ordered his favorit architect François Cuvilliès the Amalienburg. All together five generations of Wittelsbachs took care of the Castle and Park, between 1664 and 1757, and the result was worth the effort! Other figures: The front of the Castle is 700 m long, the Park almost three square kilometers.

Castle Nymphenburg [113], Stone Hall

Castle Nymphenburg [113], ceiling frescoes in the Stone Hall

The visit starts normally in the central section, with the excellent restored **Stone Room**, a two stores high room with a great ceiling fresco (architect Cuvilliès, painter J. B. Zimmermann).

In the south wing we find the "**Gallery of Beauties**" of Ludwig I, the king selected himself 36 "beautiful women" of Munich and the royal painter Joseph Stieler portrayed them (1827-50). These include the "sweet"

Helene Sedlmayr and the "crazy" Lola Montez, who contributed to the downfall of the King in 1848.

Taking the great outside staircase in the back we arrive to the Park, its first section being the Grand Parterre, this layout with the straight middle axis reminds us of the original French style used.

Attractions in the park are the Big and small lakes with the canal ending in a waterfall and, of course, the pavilions. Among all of them the pearl is the little hunting lodge **Amalienburg**; the Elector Karl Albrecht had it built by François Cuvilliès 1734-39 for his wife Amalie Maria.

The circular Hall of Mirrors with silver ornament is a jewel of Rococo architecture, the kitchen decorated with blue Dutch tiles enchants the female visitors.

Following the signs along the park they direct us to the Badenburg, the first heated indoors bath in Europe after the Roman empire (1718-21) and to the Pagodenburg, named so after the Chinese Room in the first floor decorated with enamel paintings and silk (1717-19).

The path leading back to the Castle passes by the Hermitage of Mary Magdalena (Magdalenenklause), a feint ruin whit a grotto chapel, where the Elector Max Emanuel retired to meditate and pray (1725-28).

Last station of our Park stroll could be the Orangerie with the Glass House; here you can enjoy a drink in the cafeteria in the Palm Tree Garden.

Castle Nymphenburg [113],
Gallery of Beauties

Some museums use part of the Castle rooms, for example the **Marstall Museum** displaying a collection of ceremonial carriages, sleighs, harnesses and saddlers that recalls the heyday of the Wittelsbachs.

Specially impressive are the Crowning carriage of the short time ruling Kaiser Karl VII and the splendid sleigh of Ludwig II, that he used to reach his castles in the Bavarian Alps in winter (mostly on night trips).

The **Nymphenburg Bäuml Porcelain Museum** on the first floor comprise around 1200 historic porcelain pieces spanning from the Rococo style (Bustelli) till the Art Nouveau.

On the opposite north wing of the Castle is the **Museum of Mankind and Nature**. With modern pedagogical methods the exhibitions inform about the history of the Earth and Nature as about the evolution of animals and human beings.

Dedicated mostly to the youngest public.

Opening hours for Castle Nymphenburg and Amalienburg: Daily 9 a.m. - 6 p.m. Thu - 8 p.m. October to March daily 10 a.m. - 4 p.m. Badenburg, Pagodenburg, Hermitage of Magdalena from October to March closed. Marstall Museum, Porcelain Museum: Daily 10 a.m. - 12 a.m., 1 p.m. - 5p.m., October to March - 4 p.m. Museum of Mandkind and Nature: Daily 9 a.m. - 5 p.m. Tram 17; Bus 41. Telephone 179 08/0.

Castle Nymphenburg [113], Hall of Mirrors in the Amalienburg

Other sights of interest

Egyptian Art Museum [114]

Admirers of the Pharaoh Empire do not have to flight immediately to Cairo to enjoy the remains of the Ancient Egypt.

On one side of the Hofgarten [20] a high level collection awaits you with surprising treasures, from the prehistoric to the classical epochs, along with the pre-Christian times and the Coptic art works of the Nile valley.

An obelisk in front of the Festsaalbau of the Residence [18] marks the entrance.

> **i** Tue - Fri 9 a.m. - 5 p.m. Tue too 7 p.m. - 9 p.m. Sat, Sun 10 a.m. - 5 p.m. Mon closed. Residence, Hofgartenstreet 1. U-Bahn Odeonsplatz. Tel. 29 85 46

Allianz Arena [112]

Not finished yet and already an attraction for many, who cannot wait: the polemic Allianz-Arena, the football stadium where the opening game of the World Championship of 2006 should take place. 66 000 covered seats, 2000 business seats, 100 tribunes will cost 280 mill. Euros, added to them 185 millions should go for the infrastructure like accesses, public transportation etc. It is not a surprise to know that not all the people are fascinated by it, taking into account that the budget will be exceeded. The positive part is the futuristic design "Swimming belt" of the architect team Herzog-de Meuron with their changing lights effect.

Who would like to visit the building site must just hold tight to the cranes!

> **i** U-Bahn Fröttmaning (U 6 Garching-Hochbrück)

Alpine Museum [115]

Located on a beautiful island in the Isar river the German Alpine Association has chosen an extraordinary spot for the House of Alpinism. The Museum shows paintings and exhibits of all type from the History of Alpinism since 1760 till nowadays. In place is to be found the rich central library of the Association DAV. Interesting special exhibitions.

> **i** Tu - Fri 1 p.m. - 6 p.m. Sat, Sun 11 a.m. - 6 p.m. Mon closed. Praterinsel 5. U-Bahn Lehel; Tram 17. Tel. 21 12 24 - 0

Palaeontology Museum [116]

The interesting museum focuses in pre-historic times. If you are interested in the early past of Bavaria (stone-, bronze-, caveages, the Celts, the Romans, the Merovinger and Carolinger) will surely find here enough information. The building is in the vicinities of the Bavarian National Museum [105].

> **i** Daily 9 a.m. - 4.30 p.m. Mon closed. Lerchenfeldstr. 2. U-Bahn Lehel; Tram 17. Tel. 211 24 02

Bavaria and the Hall of Fame [117]

In the upper part of the Theresienwiese, locally known as "Wiesn", where once a year the largest Folkloric feast in the world – the "Oktoberfest" – takes place, stands the enormous statue of Bavaria, a German colossal woman dressed with a bear fur, crowned with laurel and holding a sword, with the Bavarian lion at her feet. Based on designs of Klenze/Schwanthaler, it was cast in bronze by Ferdinand von Miller and Stiglmaier in 1843 - 50; six pieces ensambled together, 18 meters high, 1560 centner weight, at the time of its erection was a technical challenge. A climb up the interior staircase to the head is rewarded by the view over the Theresienwiese and the city.

> Daily 9 a.m. - 6 p.m. Thu till 8 p.m. Mid October till end March closed.

The Hall of Fame (Ruhmeshalle) on top of the natural hill behind the Bavaria was built in 1843 - 53 by Klenze, a threewinged marble Hall in Doric style. In the back marble busts of 77 prominent Bavarians from Martin Schongauer to Ludwig Thoma.

Bavaria Film Studios [118]

Before you stuff the kids with churches and museums you should visit the Bavaria Film Studios in Geiselgasteig, the "Hollywood by the Isar".

For 1 1/2 hours with the Film-Express children and adults can feel the magic of cinema, ride the back of the worm of the Neverending story, feel claustrophobia in the submarine of Buchheim´s Boot, shiver in the Snake´s nest, astonish the stunts and the special effects.

In short: over 80 years – foundation 1919 – of Film History with famous directors (Orson Welles, Hitchcock, Fassbinder) and stars of the size of Liz Taylor, Sophia Loren, Romy Schneider, Hans Albers or Burt Lancaster. Guided tours.

Bavaria and the Hall of Fame [117]

> From March till Oct 9 a.m. - 5 p.m., from Nov till Feb 10 a. m. - 3 p.m. Bavaria-Filmplatz 7. Tram 25. Tel. 64 99 23 04

Castle Blutenburg [119]

Castle Blutenburg [119]

In the vicinities of the Motor-way exit Obermenzing – and still an oasis of peace and tran-quility: a former castle chapel (1488) enlarged by the Duke Sigismund in the outskirts of town transformed in to a Hunting and Water Castle surroun-ded by the river Würm.

A jewel of late Gothic style with rich filigran altars; the painting are work of Jan Polack from Cra-kovia, a master of the Munich late Gothic. The (almost too per-fectly) restored castle homes the International Youth Library,

↩ *Castle Blutenburg [119]*

a memorial to the writer Erich Kästner, a concert Hall and a restaurant. It is worthy to make the long way.

> **i** Seldweg 15, Blutenburg.
> S-Bahn Pasing, Bus 73

BMW-Hochhaus and Museum [111]

Walking distance from the Olympic grounds is the BMW-Hochhaus and the BMW Mu-seum [111]. The unusual archi-tectural construction with the form of four cylinders grouped around an open shaft (design Karl Schwanzer, 1970-73) are the headquarters of the adminis-tration of BMW.

In contrast to it the windowless, silver-colored concrete bowl houses the Museum. The exhibi-tion Zeithorizonte traces the ma-jor developments in the history of BMW stretching back almost 80 years. Which is the develop-

BMW Museum [111]

ment of the values of work, factory, electronics, environment, free time- and which is the role that the human being plays in it? With help of visual technologies such as 100 films, videos and slides cast light on developments and visions.

> ℹ️ Daily 9 a.m. - 5 p.m.
> Petuelring 130. U-Bahn
> Olympiazentrum; several
> Bus lines. Tel. 38 22 -33 07.

Botanical Garden [120]

BMW Museum [111],
Exhibition "Zeithorizonte"

Botanical Garden [120]

You could link the visit of this 20 Ha exhibition ground with the one of the Castle Nymphenburg and park. This garden is one of the most attractive in Europe as it fulfills the expectations of the scientists and the amateurs. Following the signs you come through the most im-

portant sectors (e. g. the decoration yard, the genetic and ecologic section, the rhododender plantations, the Alpinum, the glass house).

> Daily 9 a.m. - 6 p.m. winter 5 p.m. Glass houses 9 a.m. - 11.45 a.m., 1 p.m. - 5.30 p.m. winter 4 p.m. Menzinger Str. 65. U-Bahn Rotkreuzplatz; Tram 17. Tel. 178 61-351

German Museum [9]

German Museum [9], Fischer-Ewer MARIA HF-31, 1880

German Museum [9]

This museum, one of the largest scientific and technical museum in the world, was founded in 1903 by Oskar von Miller, but opened the doors in 1925. The extended building on the island on the Isar has an exhibition area of 50 000 square meters, about 15 000 exhibits visited per year by around 1,4 million people.

Not the only, but indeed the major reason for being so attractive: the museum offers "technology to get to grips", plenty of the demonstrative installs can be operated with a button or a handle, this working models are mostly used by the children, the not so young ones enjoy mostly the historic old timer cars, the planes, and the lifelike recreations (the Altamira caves, a coal mine).

With the passing of time has been constantly changed and enlarged. For the anniversary year 2003 parts of the exhibitions have moved to the Theresienhöhe. The accessible general library (no lend) has grown to 870 000 books.

German Museum [9], The children's empire

German Museum [9],
Transportation center

German Museum [9], aviation
and spaceflight section

German Museum [9],
Ray demonstrative model

The headquarters on the Museum Island

The classical sections are here, engines, street, bridge and water constructions, electricity, physic, chemistry, the legendary coal mine; the fascinating boat and planes section, an unexpected beautiful collection of musical instruments, the newest developments in atomic physics, electronics, automatism, computers and information technologies.

Due to the partial moving to the Theresienwiese the rooms left free are dedicated to the Center for New Technologies – with emphasis on Genetic and Nano technology as well as Software.

Apart from this a new exhibition for children is planned: "Das Kinderreich".

> ℹ Daily 9 a.m. - 5 p.m.
> Wed a chosen section
> till 8 p.m.
> Museumsinsel 1.
> S-Bahn Isartor; Tram 18.
> Telephone 2179-433

The Transport center in the Theresienhöhe

Three big exhibition tents are devoted to the new Transport Center of the German Museum since the anniversary of 2003 with the title "work in progress". Emphasis on: City traffic, traveling, mobility and technology.

Here the unique collection of transport items will be presented from a new point of view.

The second part of the project should be finished by 2005.

> ℹ Daily 9 a.m. - 5 p.m.
> Theresienhöhe. U-Bahn
> Schwanthaler Höhe

The Hangar Schleißheim

The aviation Museum is located in the north outskirts of town, in the restored historic hangar (built 1912-19) and complements with 8000 square meters exhibition grounds the aviation and spaceflight sections of the main house.

A permanent exhibition is dedicated to the "vertical take-off".

> ℹ Daily 9 a.m. - 5 p.m.
> Effnerstreet 18, Schleißheim,
> next to the castles. S-Bahn
> Oberschleißheim; Bus 292.

Amazeum [121]

The "Center for Nature and Technology" in the former Fairs' center of the German Museum is the successor of the Forum der Technik.

After its complete renovation major attractions are the IMAX-Cinema, bringing the spectator close to Nature in an unusual way with the 16 x 22 m big screen, the other cinemas and the most modern Planetarium in the world, other are still projects as the Adventure center named The Gate to Knowledge.

The changing exhibitions program can be checked in the newspapers or through telephonic information.

> ℹ Daily 9 a.m. - 11 p.m.
> Museumsinsel 1. S-Bahn
> Isartor. Tel. Ticket booking
> 211 25-180, Program
> information 211 25-183

Müllersches Volksbad [10]

Even if you forgot your bathing suit, you should at least take a look to it. Sponsored by the Munich citizen Karl Müller, built in 1897-1901 by the architect Hocheder, was at its time the most modern indoors swimming pool in Europe. It was, and still is, the "most beautiful Art Nouveau pool in Europe". The access to the opulent decorated Swimming Halls are allowed only to bathers. Nevertheless you can get a good idea of the whole by the entrance halls, the cafeteria and the exterior (check the remarkable tower!).

> i Daily 7.30 a.m. - 23 p.m.,
> Big Hall Mon - 5 p.m. Rosenheimer Str. 1 (by the Ludwigsbridge). S-Bahn Isartor; Tram 18. Tel. 23 61-34 34

City Coin Museum [122]

The collection in the Hofdamenstock in the Residence [18] is unfairly not given the importance that it is worth.

With about 2500 exhibits (more variety rests in the cellars) is the largest of this kind in Germany and owns as well the most extensive library to Numismatic and History of Money.

> i Tu, Wed, Fri, Sat, Sun 10
> a.m. - 5 p.m., Thu 10 a.m. -
> 7 p.m. Mon closed.
> Entrance Residenzstreet 1.
> U-Bahn Odeonsplatz;
> Tram 19. Tel. 22 72 21

The Olympia-Park and the Olympic-Stadium [110]

The north part of the city gained in attractive thanks to the 20th Summer Olympic Games. The **Olympia Park** [110], built from 1968 after the plans of the architects Behnisch and partners, was laid out on the grounds of the former first airport of Munich. It turned to be the most beautiful sport park one could imagine to the pleasure of the people in Munich.

The highlights of this almost 3 square-kilometers area are the 52-meter-hill, the with alpine vegetation covered Olympiaberg, made of rubbles of the bombed city; an artificial lake, fed by the Nymphenburger canal and the group of sport buildings: the **Olympic Stadium**, the Olympic Hall and the Olympic Swimming Pool with the legendary net-like roof, which set new standards for the architecture of the century.

The daring construction of the acrylic-tiled-roof is held by 12 big Pillars 81 meters high and 36 smaller ones. Added to these we find the Olympic Ice Stadium with an open air skating ground, and the Small Olympic Hall, the former Bicycle Race Stadium.

Everything "peered down" by the 289 m. height **Olympic Tower (Olympia- und Fernsehturm)**. Two elevators bring the visitors, with a speed of 7 m / sec, up to two platforms of 189 and 192 meters altitude.

On a clear day the view reaches from Dachstein to Säntis, an alpine panorama spanning 400 km!

In the restaurant below you can combine sitting down both, the enjoyment of the view, with eating and drinking, as the revolving platform provides a complete bird's eye-view of the city every hour or so.

> **i** Olympia Park open to the public. Olympic Stadium daily 8.30 a.m. - 6 p.m., winter time 9 a.m. - 4.30 p.m. – Olympic Tower daily 9 a.m. - 12 p.m. (last ascention 11.30 p.m. restaurant from 11 a.m.). Visitors "Info-Pavillon" at the Eissportzentrum. U-Bahn Olympiazentrum; several Bus lines. Tel. 30 67 - 24 14.

Schlachthofquarter

Schwabing [103], Haidhausen, Gärtnerplatz- [6] und Glockenbachquarter have more or less lost their unique atmosphere. Probably the only ones that keep their ancestral originality are the areas between the Schlachthof, Südbahnhof and Großmarkthalle, around the Zenettiplatz, Kapuziner- and Dreimühlenstreet, known as well as the Isarvorstadt. Among the large number of locals, some international, the one to mention is the Wirtshaus am Schlachthof

with a mixture of cultures from rock to cabaret. Here had his premiere the popular Otfried Fischer before the serial "Der Bulle von Tölz" made him famous.

> **i** U-Bahn Poccistrasse

Siemens Forum [123]

A permanent exhibition "the milestones and visions of the Siemens evolution" in the fields of microelectronics, communication and information technology, creation and transmission of energy, automatism, transport technology, and electronic medicine. Changing exhibitions go in depth in the different fields. The building itself is well worth attention, design by the famous architect Richard Meier, responsible of the Getty Museum in Los Angeles too.

> **i** Daily 9 a.m. - 5 p.m. Sat closed. Oskar-von-Miller-Ring 20. U-Bahn Odeonsplatz; Bus 53. Tel. 089 - 63 63 26 60

Siemens Forum

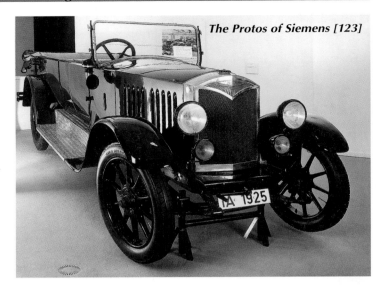

The Protos of Siemens [123]

St. Anna im Lehel [124]

Architectonic prelude to Rococo in Munich and Old Bavaria. This convent church was built up to celebrate the birth of the future Elector Max III Joseph, by Joh. Michael Fischer 1727-33, decorated with a ceiling frescoe by Cosmas Damian Asam – The Saints in Heaven- and sculptures and frescoes by J. B. Straub and Egid Quirin Asam.

The interior transmits a very equilibrated feeling thanks to the oval shape central room which set standards. The façade integrates discreet in the whole ensemble of the convent.

This church mostly destroyed during the war serves as example of creation in the reconstruction of memorials (architect Erwin Schleich).

St. Michael in Berg by Laim [125]

In this quarter, where hardly tourists can be found, hides a precious jewel of the Bavarian Rococo. The constructor was a Wittelsbach, though not the Elector, but his brother Clemens August, Archbishop (and Elector as well) of Cologne, he ordered the church to Joh. Michael Fischer in one of his local market places. It was finished in 1758.

The church is well worth importance having one of the most beautiful, cheerful and serene interiors of the 18th century.

The decoration with frescoes and stucco is work of Johann Baptist Zimmermann, the altars, angels and saints of J. B. Straub.

ℹ Sankt-Anna-Platz 21.
U-Bahn Lehel

ℹ Clemens-August-Street 9a. U-Bahn Michaeli-Bad; Tram 19

Ethnological Museum (Staatl. Museum für Völkerkunde) [126]

A great collection of artefacts from diverse national groups, specially from Africa, Mid and South America, East Asia and Oceania. Coming from the "chamber of Wonders" of the Wittelsbach, a sort of odds room.

The visit can concentrate in an specific sector. Well worth a visit are the changing exhibitions (Nepal, Yemen etc.), attracting a great number of visitors.

> **i** Tu - Sun 9.30 a.m - 5.15 p.m. Maximilianstreet 42. U-Bahn Lehel; S-Bahn Isartor; Tram 17, 19. Tel. 21 01 36 -100

South cemetery [127]

Not only in Paris and Vienna a visit to a cemetery has charm. A contemplative stroll through the south cemetery in Munich makes us meet the last resting place of lots of prominents (Spitzweg, Senefelder, Gabelsberger, Rottmann, Kaulbach, Fraunhofer, Klenze, Ohm etc.).

> **i** Entrance Thalkirchner Street 17. U-Bahn Sendlinger Tor.

Hellabrunn Zoo [128]

In a big 70 hectars triangular shaped ground in the south of Munich, between the Isar and the high bank, with lots of green and water, there the animals they can feel like at home. 5000 animals of around 400 different species are gathered here and show (not always) their best side.

Since the foundation of the zoo there has been lots of changes, beginning with the elephant house, the big birds cage with the 5000 square meters hanging net construction, the new pavilions for the apes and the deep frozen Polarium for the polar bears, the penguins and the seals.

Lots of work has been done in the fields of the retroactive breeding of already non-existing animals like the primitive Ox or wild Mustangs, or the maintenance of species in danger of extinction like the wild duck, brown bears, leopards and others with little chances of survival in open nature. In the vicinities of the entrance: a domestic animals zoo and pony riding.

> **i** Daily 9 a.m. - 5 p.m. Siebenbrunner Street 6 (Thalkirchen). U-Bahn 3; Bus 52. Tel. 625 080

Memorial "white Rose" [101]

In the atrium of the Ludwig-Maximilians-University [101] is to be found the exhibition, information room and library in memory of the resistance movement of the sisters Scholl.

They distributed leaflets at the university, observed as against the Nazi regime, denounced and executed by the Nazis in 1943.

> Mon - Fri 10 a.m. - 4 p.m.
> Geschwister-Scholl-Platz.
> U-Bahn Universität.
> Tel. 21 80 - 30 53

ZAM – Center for Unusual Museums [129]

A unique concentration in the world of seven "unusual" collections under one roof.

Museum of perfume, Sissi Museum (to the memory of the empress Elisabeth of Austria), chamber pot Museum, toy car Museum, Bourdalou Museum, Easter bunny Museum.

> Daily 10 a.m. - 6 p.m.
> Westenriederstreet 41.
> S-Bahn Isartor; Tram 17, 18.
> Tel. 290 41 21

Excursions from Munich

In the North: Schleißheim, Dachau, Freising

The north of Munich is more charming and interesting as you might think when leaving the city. To arrive to **Schleißheim** you can drive along the Ingolstädter Strasse (B 13) or take the suburbs train "Flughafenlinie" S 1. The three Palaces and the large garden grounds create an impressive ensemble, perfect example of the court architecture and gardening art of the 17th and 18th century.

The **Old Palace** is a relatively modest country mansion of the end of the 16th century for the Duke Wilhelms V. His successor, Maximilian I, enlarged it in

Palace Schleißheim

1616-23 following the Italian Renaissance style and making it more comfortable and generous. After having been severely damaged during the war was provisionally rebuilt and houses today different exhibitions.

The **New Palace** is the result of the obsession for recognition of a Bavarian prince, who overestimated his own possibilities with the posterior consequences for his country.

Prince Elector Max Emanuel, "The blue prince", defeated in his youth the Turks and considered himself chosen for great deeds, wanted to build here his Bavarian "Versailles".

He abused of the finances and

Palace Schleißheim

335 meters length is the central wing, enlarged with 2 side wings and corner pavilions. The big windows, allowing the light in, open to the west, direction the Old Palace and to the east looking over the park.

The interior of the palace has been recently renovated, specially the masterpiece staircase (finished one century later by Klenze) as the voluptuous frescoes and stucco work of Cuvilliès, J. B. Zimmermann and the brothers Asam. The predominant scenes of the rooms relate the triumph over the Turks and the General responsible of it!

What we are really thankful for is for the great collection of paintings that Max Emanuel gathered together. The Grand

that lead him to his political margination and the long term exile. The bombastic project had to reduce costs, which was only positive. This way the construction began in 1701 by Zuccalli and was finished in 1726 by Joseph Effner resulting in a buoyant Memorial to the late Bavarian Baroque and Rococo.

Gallery in the first floor was one of the first Painting Galleries in Europe. Now a branch of the Baroque Bavarian State Collection of Paintings is exhibit here with important works of the Flemish, Italian and French schools, among others Peter Paul Rubens, Anthonis van Dyck and other great masters.

The **Palace Park**, stretching between the New and the Old Palace, was laid out in 1720 following the rules of the French Park-master Le Notre.

Together with the Herrenhausen Palace by Hannover, is the only Baroque garden in Germany that has kept the strict geometrical style.

Palace Lustheim was built between 1684-88 by Enrico Zuccalli as a living and hunting Palace in court late Baroque style.

This palace contains the precious **Ernst Schneider Collection of Meissen Porcelain**; it comprises around 1800 pieces from the flourishing times of the Manufactory Meißen in the 18th century, among others works of Böttger, Chinese pieces by Hörold and animal figurines by Kändler, until the porcelain of the time of the Seven Years War.

> **i** New Palace and Baroque gallery, Palace Lustheim with Collection of Meißen Porcelain : Tu - Sun 9 a.m. - 6 p.m. (April to September), 10 a.m. - 4 p.m. (October to March). S 1, Oberschleißheim. Tel. 089-315 87 20

You can reach **Dachau** either with the suburbs train, or driving along the Dachauer Strasse (B 304), 17 km. The name of the city is synonym for the terror regime of the Nazis, and will remain such for a long time.

Though the history and life of Dachau does not depend on this: almost 1200 years ago a Wittelsbach castle was built here, and in the 16th century transformed in a proud Renaissance palace, reconstructed in 1715 as the summer residence of the Bavarian Prince Electors.

The southwest wing contains the representative Festivity Hall with one of the most beautiful

Palace Lustheim

Renaissance wooden roofs remaining to the north of the Alps. The view from the Palace terrace to Munich and the Alps in background in a clear day (for example with Föhn) makes already the excursions worthy.

In the 19th century Dachau became an attractive place for artists, among others Carl Spitzweg, Wilhelm Leibl, Max Liebermann and Lovis Corinth painted here. In the Paintings Gallery opposite the City Hall [2] plenty of works of this time are to bee seen. In Dachau found the young attorney Ludwig Thoma the "Model" of the old Bavarian society, which gave his works the characteristic tone and form.

> Verkehrsverein, Konrad-Adenauer-Street 2,
> 85221 Dachau,
> Tel. 08131-75286.

The **Concentration Camp** (KZ-Gedenkstätte) is located on the east boundaries of town, in 1933, the in those days Munich Police chief, Heinrich Himmler ordered the construction of the first concentration camp in Germany, which served as model for the following ones.

Over 200 000 people entered the camp's gates, more than 32 000 died due to torture, execution, famine and infections.

Still standing there the entrance gate with the cynical inscription "Arbeit macht frei" (Freedom through work) and the crematorium, two shacks had been reconstructed. Entrance is free, no reservation is needed.

There are guided tours (aprox. 2 1/2 hours) and short introductions (aprox. 30 minutes). Twice a day a documentary film is shown in German and English. In the honor cemetery in Etzenhauser Leite stands a Memory Chapel dedicated to the mostly unknown prisoners. On the north side of the concentration camp stands the monastery of the Carmelit order Holly Blood Dachau.

> Daily except Mon 9 a.m. - 5 p.m. Alte Römerstreet 75, 85221 Dachau. S 2 Dachau, with Bus 724 (KZ Gedenkstätte Parking) and with Bus 726 (KZ-Gedenkstätte Main entrance). Tel. 08131-669970

Freising, 33 km north from Munich on the shores of the Isar, to be reached with suburb train, by car along Freimann (B 11) or taking the A 9 direction Airport, is actually older than Munich, and an unwillingly helper of the foundation of the former. Here worked already the bishop St. Bonifatius (founder of the bishopric in 739) and St. Korbinian (first bishop and city patron).

Their successor brought the bishopric to grow in importance. It was in 1158 that the Duke Heinrich the Lion destroyed the toll bridge by Föhring and moved the salt trade road to the south; this took away an important money source meanwhile the growth of the new founded city of Munich started.

The skyline of Freising is dominated by the five halls Romanesque **Cathedral** on top of the hill Domberg, the third construction on the spot (1160-1205), which in the early 18th century received new eccentric stucco and frescoes decoration from the hands of the Asam brothers. The crypt, an original from

1160, is very interesting, 24 pillars hold the vault, one of them decorated with twisted bodies of human beings and monsters, the so called "Bestiensäule".

Here rest as well, in the relic shrine, the body of St. Korbinian.

On the same hill, and built in 1345 the Benedictine Church, where now the **Diocesan Museum** shows with 10 000 objects the history of the Bishopric of Freising, the largest Religious museum in Germany, and the Elector Bishop Residence with a nice Renaissance arcade court (1519). Today a spiritual education centre (Kardinal-Döpfner-Haus).

Freising with 36 000 inhabitants is not only a spiritual place. The **Bürgerstadt** at the foot of the hill, the "lower town" boasts with activity and commercial life, around the Market square and the Gothic parish church of St. Georg (around 1400) and the restored patrician houses.

They are not short in cafes and restaurants. The bier served in those comes probably from not far away: the former, founded in 725, Benedictine monastery Weihenstephan where now the Bavarian State Brewery Weihenstephan is housed, is the oldest brewery in the world and nowadays part of the Technical University of Munich with the Brewing Faculty.

The worldwide good reputation is shared by the beers and the educated brew masters with the same origin. The quality of the bier can be checked out in the bier garden or in the Bierstüberl of the brewery itself.

> **i** Fremdenverkehrsamt,
> Marienplatz 7,
> 85354 Freising;
> Tel. 08161-54122.

Museum Buchheim

In the south: the five lakes district

If Munich is one of the most attractive cities in Germany is due in part to its location, the proximity to the lakes and mountains in the south. The five lakes district is still to be reached with the suburbs train – end stations Starnberg and Herrsching-; the Starnberg lake is nicknamed the "Tub of Munich", the shores of the other small lakes – Wörthsee, Pilsensee, Weßlinger See – are spotted with weekend houses and camping places (which by the way is not of the liking of everyone).
Although the connections with public transportation are good, for the day excursion we recommend a car.

The **Starnberg Lake** fills a former glacier basin enclosed by a morrene mound, and offers in its 20 km length, 2 – 5 km wide and up to 123 m depth, facilities to all kind of water sports, specially sailors and surfers. This is our first destination: Following the A 95 / A 952 direction Starnberg, shortly before, in Percha we turn in to the Ostuferstraße to the **Castle Berg**. Here stands since the 17th century a summer residence of the Wittelsbach with a large park. Berg was the last place to see King Ludwig II alve, the spot in the lake where he died in a mysterious way with his companion Dr. Gudden (13. 6. 1886), is marked with a Cross. On the shores you can find a Votive chapel in pseudo-Gothic style. From Berg to the south the road along the lake is closed to the traffic (something of the liking of the cyclists and pedestrians), there are nevertheless other access roads to reach the villages of Ammerland and Ambach. The minority lucky enough to live or to own a little beach here (if possible with private house) belongs to a closed society. A good address to have a little bite: Gasthaus Fischmeister in Ambach, house ,by the way, of the actors family Bierbichler. **Seeshaupt** at the very south end of the lake is the turning round point for the excursion boats, owns several beaches and a well worth seeing church with Romanesque foundations (St. Michael). South from Seeshaupt we reach the Natural Protected Area Osterseen, 21 beautiful moors together, very often non accessible at all.

Once on the lively west shore of the lake we can only travel north, next place Seeseiten (simple restaurant) towards **Bernried**, an idyllic village among the fruit gardens. Here an Augustinian convent was founded already in 1120, the actual church dates back to 1663. In contrast to it, just 100 meters away along the shores, we face back the modern times with the **Buchheim Museum of Fantasy!**

We find here the legendary collection of Expressionism of this polemic multi talented man Lothar-Günther Buchheim (Bestseller author, Photographer, editor of art and children books), together with handicraft objects, Bavarian Folk art and objects from all over the world.

> **i** April to October Mon - Fri 10 a.m. - 6 p.m. Sat, Sun 10 a.m. - 8 p.m.; November to March Tue - Fri 10 a.m. - 5 p.m. Sat, Sun 10 a.m. - 6 p.m. Am Hirschgarten 1, 82347 Bernried; Tel. 0 8158 - 99 70 60

Passing by Tutzing, the second largest place by the lake, with the former palace housing today the well known Evangelist Academy, we reach the Aristocratic Villas place of **Feldafing**. They are very proud to own the beautiful (18 holes) golf course as well as the Hotel Kaiserin Elisabeth, the place where the Empress "Sissi" spent 22 summers, not far away from the "parents' house" Castle Possenhofen. In front of the place the romantic Roses island, where Sissi, in a honourable way, used to meet her cousin Ludwig, the later "Fairy tales king". After passing Possenhofen, which castle can be seen only from outside, and the long stretched outdoors activities ground of the city of Munich (including a beach) we arrive to Pöcking and immediately afterwards to Starnberg, capital of the province and "lake-metropolis" with a beautiful shore promenade. Evil tongues say from Starnberg to be "the richest and ugliest city in Bavaria".

Following the street signs indicating towards Herrsching, we end up in a comfortable national road over the hill Höhenrücken, separating the Ammersee from the Starnberger lake. Pretty soon we will catch the first glimpse of the steeple of the

Andechs Monastery. It was in this place where in 1438, after the discovery of a relics treasure, an Augustinian collegiate was founded. Later transformed in a Benedictine convent, whose monks knew how to make out of their place the most important pilgrimage place in all Bavaria. The location of the Holly Hill providing a fantastic view over the Alps in the south could only contribute to the success. Nowadays there are pilgrims coming to admire not only the gracious image of the Mother of God (around 1500), but those who come to sample the strong bear brewed by the Benedictine monks who call Andechs home, in the brewery, the bier garden or in the restaurant of the monastery.

We recommend, before the effects of the sparkling liquid affects our sight, to have a look inside the **Monastery church**: The Gothic Hall church interior was transformed in 1750 in to a sumptuous Rococo place thanks to the hands of J. B. Zimmermann (Stucco and Frescoes) and J. B. Straub (statues of the altar). The visit of the precious relics treasure (booking required), theater performances and concerts bring life to the inside. The church tower, visible from a long distance, can not be climbed.

Below the Holly Hill stretches the third largest lake of Bavaria – 18 km. long, up to 5 km wide- the **Ammersee**. In contrast with the "flashy" Starnberger lake still offers a little rustic feeling, despite the influences of the people from Munich and on the west shore from Augsburg. From the village of Erling below Andechs we drive leaving Herrsching to the right, the very popular south shore of the lake with the Protected Bird Area, proceeding to **Dießen**, in many ways the most important town on the west shore: originally a fisherman place, later "ennobled" by the spiritual center of the Augustinian collegiate in 1132, later on home of artists and above all handicraft people (painters, musicians, pottery).

Take a walk through the neat marketplace and along the shores of the lake and you will not be disappointed! Together with Andechs a landmark of the Ammersee, to be seen from the distance, the **Marienmünster** (Convent church of St. Marien), a fantastic work of the Rococo master architect Johann Michael Fischer (1732-39), wonderful interiors by J. G. Bergmüller (Ceiling frescoe "The Heaven of Dießen"), Ignaz Günt-her as the stucco specialist of Wessobrunn Feichtmair and Üblherr. – The view to the north closes with the "Winter church" St. Stephan with beautiful sculptures from the Romanic and Gothic times.

> **i** Tourist info:
> Fremdenverkehrsamt,
> Mühlstreet 4a, 86911
> Dießen: Tel. 0 88 07-1048

We continue along the west shore direction north. The villages on our way **(Riederau, Holzhausen, Utting, Schondorf),** with the passing of time transformed in Villas colonies, still offer a quaint and cozy atmosphere unique to Bavarian towns, at least during the week days: they all invite to stay, to stroll along the lakeside, to pick up a beach or look for a terrace, to jump in a rented boat… We can recommend two restaurants: the Seehaus in Riederau with good food and nice view, and the Alte Villa in Utting, not only for gourmets, but for the Jazz lovers too. – The only "sightseeing": the formerly Romanic chapel St. Jakob back to the 12th century in Unterschondorf (Seekapelle). – **Stegen** at the very north end of the lake is not only the "Main port" of the Ammersee fleet. Here we find the access to the motorway (A 96 Lindau), which takes us back to Munich in the quickest way. The total distance covered by the excursion, depending on the side trips, 120-150 km. Another possibility to get to know the Five Lakes Area: A boat trip on the Starnberg or the Ammersee lake, well worth with nice weather!

> **i** Info-Tel. 08151-120 23 and
> 8061 (Starnberger See),
> 0 81 43 - 940 21 (Ammersee).

Monastery Andechs

Where to stay in Munich

Munich has enough luxurious and first class hotels. A little more difficult is to find accommodation for the small pocket. Therefore we begin with the simplest ones.

Camping places
(from March to October)

- ➲ "Langwieder See", Eschenrieder Strasse 119, Telephone 864 15 66
- ➲ "Thalkirchen", Zentralländstrasse 49, Telephone 723 17 07
- ➲ "Obermenzing", Lochhauser Strasse 59, Telephone 811 22 35

Youth hostels

- ➲ DJH-Gästehaus, Miesingstrasse 4, Telephone 723 65 60
- ➲ DJH München, Wendl-Dietrich-Strasse 20, Telephone 13 11 56
- ➲ DJH Pullach (Isartal), Burg Schwaneck, Telephone 793 0643
- ➲ CVJM, Landwehrstrasse 13, Telephone 552 1410
- ➲ Haus International, Elisabeth-strasse 87, Telephone 12 00 60

Hotels from 50 to 100 Euro
(per night/person with breakfast)

- ➲ Adria – nice pension in Lehel. Liebigstrasse 8a, 80538. Tel. 24 21 17-0, Fax 24 21 17-999. S-Bahn Isartor
- ➲ Blauer Bock – charming traditional hotel near the Viktualienmarkt [5]. Sebastiansplatz 9, 80331. Tel. 089-23 17 80, Fax 23 17 82 00. U/S-Bahn Marienplatz
- ➲ Dachs [103] – cheap address in Schwabing, family business. Amalienstrasse 12, 81247 Tel. 089-28 20 86, Fax 28 08 29. U-Bahn Odeonsplatz
- ➲ Jagdschloss – in the northwest suburb of Obermenzing, near the Autobahn Stuttgart. Alte Allee 21, 81245. Tel. 089-82 08 20, Fax 82 08 21 00
- ➲ Leopold [103] – convenient in price and location in the outer Schwabing. Leopoldstrasse 119, 80804. Tel. 089-36 70 61, Fax 36 04 31 50. U-Bahn Münchner Freiheit

- ➲ Theresia - pension, good location for art fans (Pinakotheks!) and High school visitors (Tech. Univ.). Luisenstrasse 51, 80333. Tel. 089-52 12 50, Fax 542 06 33. U-Bahn Theresienstrasse

Hotels over 100 Euro
(per night/person with breakfast)

- ➲ An der Oper – favorite place for those who have to do, active or passive, with the opera or the theater. Falkenturmstr. 10, 80331. Tel. 089-290 02 70, Fax 29 00 27 29. U/S-Bahn Marienplatz
- ➲ Exquisit – in the vicinities of the hospital quarter. Pettenkofer-strasse 3, 80336. Tel. 551 99 00, Fax 55 19 94 99. U-Bahn Sendlinger-Tor-Platz
- ➲ Platzl Hotel – closer to the Hof-bräuhaus [12] cannot be, but it does not disturb. Sparkassenstr. 10, 80331. Telephone 089-23 70 30, Fax 23 70 38 00
- ➲ Torbräu – guests coming back are the best publicity for the house! Tal 41, 80331. Tel. 089-24 23 40, Fax 24 23 42 35. S-Bahn Isartor-platz
- ➲ Domus – location for the lovers of the Old Munich-Lehel! St.-Anna-Strasse 31, 80538. Tel. 089-22 17 04, Fax 228 53 59. U-Bahn Lehel

Hotels over 200 Euro
(per nicht/person with breakfast)

- ➲ Mandarin Oriental – small but classy, roof terrace with view over Munich. Neuturmstrasse 1, 80331. Tel. 089-29 09 80, Fax 22 25 39
- ➲ Kempinski Hotel Vier Jahreszeiten – well-tried traditional hotel. Maximilianstrasse 17, 80539. Tel. 089-212 50, Fax 21 25 20 00
- ➲ Königshof [37] – all comforts in a nice family business. Karlsplatz 25, 80335. Tel. 089-55 13 60, Fax 55 13 61 13
- ➲ Hilton Park München – nice location by the English garden. Am Tucherpark 7, 80538. Tel. 089-384 50, Fax 38 45 25 88

Where to eat in Munich

This is not a guide to the gastro-nomic temples. Whoever can or wants to afford them can find infor-mation in other places.

We do not unveil "secrets" outside in Trudering or Großhadern. Who comes to visit Munich and has time and feels like making the long way to there?

Whoever wants to eat good in the city center and at good prices will find here a list of restaurants and addresses to make him happy:

Bavarian snack

Bavarian rustic

- ➲ Andechser am Dom [31], Weinstrasse 7, by the Frauen-kirche; Telephone 29 84 81
- ➲ Augustiner-Großgaststätten, Neuhauser Strasse 27, Pedestrian area; Tel. 2318 32 57
- ➲ Zum Dürnbräu, Tal 21, corner Dürnbräugasse; Tel. 222 195
- ➲ Franziskaner Fuchsenstubn, Perusastrasse 5; Tel. 231 81 20
- ➲ Hofbräuhaus [12] - Schwemme and Biergarten, in restaurant "home cooking", Am Platzl 9; Telephone 22 16 76

Traditional "home cooking"

- ➲ Zum Alten Markt [5], Dreifaltig-keitsplatz 3, by the Viktualien-markt; Telephone 29 99 95
- ➲ Halali, Schönfeldstrasse 22; Telephone 28 59 09
- ➲ Ratskeller [1], Marienplatz 8; Telephone 089-219 98 90
- ➲ Spatenhaus an der Oper [18], Residenzstrasse 12; Telephone 089-2 90 70 60

- ➲ Zum Spöckmeier [1], Rosenstrasse 9, by Marienplatz; Telephone 26 80 88

Young, international, trendy

- ➲ Dukatz [26], for (wannabe-) intellectuals, Literaturhaus, Salvatorplatz 1; Tel. 23 91 96 00
- ➲ Eisbach – Bar & Küche, really cool, Marstallplatz 3; Telephone 22 80 17 81
- ➲ Lenbach – with the legendary catwalk, Ottostrasse 6, Telephone 5 49 13 00
- ➲ Werneckhof [103] – French cuisine in Schwabing, Werneck-strasse 11; Telephone 39 99 36
- ➲ Blaues Haus – with theater flair, Hildegardstrasse 1; Telephone 23 33 69 77

Lager wheat beer

Lager ale whit Obazda – cheese plate

Addresses, Information, Tips from A to Z

Information about the city

Postal address: Fremdenverkehrsamt, 80313 München
Tel.-Zentrale: 089-233-965 00
Fax-Zentrale: 089-233 302 33
Internet: www.muenchen-tourist.de
E-mail: tourismus@ems.muenchen.de

Information offices

• Tourist Information in main train station-Hauptbahnhof. Bahnhofplatz 2 (next to DER) Mon - Sat 9.30 a.m. - 6.30 p.m., Sun 10 a.m. - 6 p.m.
• Tourist Information in Marienplatz [1] In Neue Rathaus [2] Mon - Fri 10 a.m. - 8 p.m., Sat 10 a.m. - 4 p.m.
• Tourist Information in airport-Flughafen München main building. Mon - Fri 10 a.m. -9 p.m., Sat, Sun, Hol 12 a.m. - 8 p.m.
• Telephone-Information 24 hours. Congresses, events, trade fairs, exhibitions. Tel. 089-23 33 00 70
• Hotel telephone bookings Tel. 23 39 65 55 – Mon -Thu 9 a.m. - 5 p.m., Fri 9 a.m. - 3 p.m.
• City guides: bookings and advice Telephone 233-302 34
• Congresses and events: advice and escorting – Telephone 23 33 02 13, Fax 23 33 02 51

Arriving by car

Information: ADAC, Tel. 519 50; ADAC-telephone operator: 0180-510 11 12; ADAC City breakdown assistance, Tel. 0180-2 22 22 22 driver guide stations: at the Autobahn exits of the A 8 (Stuttgart and Salzburg) Park-&-Ride-Places: by the subway and suburb train station in the outskirts

Arriving by train

Munich main station-Hbf: terminal train station in the center, junction for all type of trains and all directions S- and U-Bahn: all S-Bahn-Lines and U-Bahn-Lines 1, 2, 4, 5 in the underground level.
Taxi-Stops: in front, left and right the main building.
Auto-ferry train: München-Ostbahnhof, Telephone 13 08 44 25 -7

Arriving by plane

Flughafen Franz-Joseph-Strauß; internat. short form MUC

Operator: 9 75 00; Flight information: 97 52 13 13

Conections city-airport:
With a car (Taxi, rental car); with the Airport-City-Bus every 20 minutes from and to train station North , over the A 9, about 45-60 minutes

With the S-Bahn: Lines S 1 and S 8; every 20 Minuten, trip to the train station takes 40 minutes

Attorneys:

Rechtsanwalt Christoph Duge & Partner, Neuhauser Str. 15, 80331 München, phone +49-89-2904433 or priv. +49-89-8505599, fax +49-89-291750, mobile +49-173-357 73 85, e-mail Christoph.Duge@t-online.de
Attorney Duge, your civil law specialist, helps in cases like car accidents, contracts and business deals, inheritance.
A criminal law expert helps in crisis situation. The law office is located at the central pedestrian zone and can be easily reached by car or public transportation.
Office hours:
weekdays 9:00 am – 6.00 pm or according to agreement

City guided tours

• Guided tours through the Fremdenverkehrsamt München:
For individuals and groups, city tours, walking tours, museums, churches, castles, etc, in 22 languages inc. for deaf visitors:
Telephone 233-302 34, 233-302 31, 233-302 04, Fax 233-303 37
• Munich city tours at different times and different programs:
Tel. 55 02 89 95, Fax 54 90 75 70
•Taxi-Guides :
for individuals and small groups (max. 7 people): Hotline 24-hours. service, Telephone 0175-481 28 48; Bookings Telephone 216 10, 194 10; Telephone 216 10, Fax 45 05 41 23
• Spurwechsel :
original city tours on foot, by bike or tram, special themes,
Telephone 692 46 99
Internet: www.spurwechsel.info
• Stattreisen :
on foot, by tram and bike, 70 themes- and city zones, different languages, Tel. 54 40 42 30, Fax 54 40 42 99

Getting around with public transport

Munich's public transportation system – (S-Bahn, U-Bahn, Tram, Bus) – is excellent, but the fare system complicated to understand. If you use the public system rarely we recomend to purchase a Streifenkarte (in the inner city validate 2 stripes!); there are single- and partner day tickets (for up to 5 people), and the same for 3 days.

Good value is the Tourist Welcome Card with extra discounts for citiy tours, museums, and monuments (available in the Tourist information office at the train station and in the Marienplatz [1]).

> **i** MVV-schedule-information:
> 41 42 43 44
> www.mvv-muenchen.de

Taxi

long distance, guide drivers, deliveries to normal fare. Mini bus up to 8 people, reservations.
Taxi-operator Tel. 21610 u. 19410;
Taxi-operator Isarfunk Tel. 45 05 40

When something happens...

Emergency
Police, radio-patroll: Telephone 110
Fire brigades, emergency doctor: 112
Emergency assistance: 55 17 71
Emergency farmacy service: 59 44 75
(More addresses in the monthly oficial program "München im...")
Lost property office:
City lost property office, Oetztaler Strasse 17, Telephone 23 34 59 00

Lost property office of the German railways, main station opposite track 26, Telephone 13 08 - 66 64

Lost property office in the Ostbahnhof (for lost in the S-Bahn-trains), Telephone 13 08 44 09

Lost property office at the airport, central hall, level 03,
Tel. 975 - 213 70, 24-hours-service

Other useful addresses

Garages and parking lots in the city center:

⊃ Am Färbergraben; open Mon - Sat 7 a.m. - 12 p.m.; entrance at Altheimer corner

⊃ Am Stachus [37]; open Mon - Sat 7 a.m. - 12 p.m., Sun and Hol 1 p.m. - 12 p.m.; entrance at Goethestr., Bayerstr., Schillerstr.

⊃ Motorama-Tiefgarage [11] at Gasteig Kulturzentrum: open 24 hours, entrance at Rosenheimer Strasse

⊃ Sicherheit-Ordner Tiefgarage am Max-Josephs-Platz [16] (by the Opera); Mon - Sat 7 a.m. - 1 a.m., Sun, Hol 1 p.m. - 1 a.m.; entrance at Maximilianstrasse

Call a Bike

Up to 2000 bikes stand between March and October next to the phoneboxes. Unlock with electronical code, payment with credit card or by standing order

Annual events

⊃ January / February: Fasching (carnival), particulary Faschingssonntag (sunday), Rosenmontag (monday), Faschingsdienstag (dance of the market woman at the Viktualienmarkt [5])

⊃ March / April: Start of the strong beer season (Starkbier)

⊃ April / May: Spingtime festivals at the Theresienwiese, Auer Dult market at the Mariahilfplatz, May beer festival

⊃ June / July: Munich film festival, Tollwood-Summer festival, Summer concerts in the Palace Nymphenburg [113] and Schleißheim, Opera season

⊃ September / October: from the third saturday in September 16 days long Oktoberfest, the largest folkloric feast in the world

⊃ October: Auer Kirchweihdult market and fair

⊃ December: Christmas markets (among others at the Marienplatz [1], at the English Garden)

Index